D0382411

J. A. ALLEN & CO.
1 Lower Grosvenor Place
London, SW1W 0EL

Specialists in
Books on
The Horse

Ride

David Broome and Steve Hadley

Ride

LEARN TO RIDE
AND LOOK AFTER YOUR HORSE

METHUEN · LONDON

First published 1984
© 1984 David Broome and Steve Hadley
Design by Christopher Holgate
Printed in Great Britain
for Methuen London Ltd
11 New Fetter Lane, London EC4P 4EE
by Hazell Watson & Viney Ltd
Member of the BPCC Group
Aylesbury, Bucks

British Library Cataloguing in Publication Data

Broome, David
    Ride.
    1. Horsemanship
    I. Title   II. Hadley, Steve
    798.2'3   SF309
    ISBN 0-413-51140-5

Contents

Acknowledgements

The authors wish to thank

Bill Pettigrew of Ettington Park Stables, Alderminster,
Warwickshire, for his help and the use of his excellent riding
school staff and pupils;

John Henshall, Alistair Shea, Clive Hiels and the following
individuals and breed societies for the book's photographs:
Farmkey Ltd for the picture on p.88; Kit Houghton for pp.127,
130 (above), 133 and 138 (above); the National Light Horse
Breeding Society for p.128; the Irish Draught Horse Society (GB)
for p.129 (above); the Cleveland Bay Horse Society for p.129
(below); the British Warm-Blood Society for p.130; Mrs D. G. de
Rivaz and the British Appaloosa Society for p.131 (below); The
Marchioness of Townshend for p.132; the Dartmoor Pony Society
for p.134; the Exmoor Pony Society for p.135; the New Forest
Pony and Cattle Breeding Society for p.136; the Shetland Pony
Stud-Book Society for p.137; the Welsh Pony and Cob Society
for p.138 (below).

Christine Bousfield for the drawings;

Sarah Dick and Tina Youngman for their patience and help
during the photo sessions;

And particularly Ann Mansbridge, the book's editor, who has
been a constant source of encouragement and invaluable help.

David Broome

Ask any 'man in the street' the question: 'With what sport do you associate the name David Broome?' Without a moment's hesitation, he would say: 'Show jumping!'

David will always be one of show jumping's favourites. He has a tremendous affection for his horses and will never overface them. It was moving to see his emotions come to the fore when his beloved Sportsman was retired during the Olympia show in 1981 – a ceremony privately arranged between his sister Mary and the organisers, involving 'smuggling' the horse into the building without David's knowledge. Although his individual achievements are enormous, he is a willing and unselfish member of British teams and has represented his country on numerous occasions.

Having Fred Broome for a father was a good start. David went more or less straight from his pram to a Shetland pony, and learned to be fiercely competitive when about three years old. He developed the will to win at a very early age, and his whole career demonstrates that single-mindedness is the key to success.

That success has been remarkable by any standards. David has been European Champion three times (a record unequalled by any other rider), and has won the King George V Gold Cup no fewer than five times – in 1968 just beating his friend and co-author of this book, Steve Hadley.

In a quarter of a century of fame and success, the names of Wildfire, Sunsalve, Mister Softee, Sportsman and Philco are most likely to remain in the minds of show jumping enthusiasts. Watch out now for Last Resort – David thinks this horse may turn out to be the best he has ever ridden.

David's two sisters are totally involved in show jumping. Liz, now married to Ted Edgar, lives in Warwickshire and is a frequent competitor in the ring. Mary, although she has ridden in the Ladies National Championship at Windsor, spends most of her time supervising the running of David's yard and patiently schooling horses.

In 1972 David turned professional, leasing horses to Esso. When this contract ended in 1975, he formed a sponsorship deal with Phil Harris of the Harris Queensway group. Phil Harris is also a great personal friend of David and plays a major part in choosing horses.

Steve Hadley

Of all George Bernard Shaw's unkind comments on a vast variety of subjects, the most famous is undoubtedly: 'Those who can, do; those who can't, teach.' He would have been a good deal less confident if he had ever met Steve Hadley, the joint author of this book. For every individual who knows him as a trainer of horses and teacher of riders, thousands have seen him as a winner in national and international competitions, and millions know him as a BBC commentator on television. There can be few people to equal Steve in the *understanding* of horses and riding, so much stressed in this book.

Surprisingly, Steve does not come from a family of dedicated equestrians. His father was thirty before he suddenly got hooked on horses, rapidly becoming a successful show jumper at county level. Six-year-old Steve took to the saddle with equal success, and was a leading British junior rider by the age of twelve.

His success on ponies was repeated on horses, and he has a remarkable list of international successes to his credit – Flying Wild, Corunna Bay and Sunorra are some of the names that readers of this book are sure to recognise. He is a member of the British Show Jumping Association's panel of instructors; his training establishment in Warwickshire is very highly regarded by those fortunate enough to be within its reach; he breeds horses for flat racing and regularly appears at the sales up and down the country.

Steve has found the ideal partner in his wife Clare, who runs the Warwickshire establishment when Steve is at the shows. She also manages to cope with their son, Ryan, who was born in 1982. Clare is herself an excellent teacher and some of her experience has found its way into the following pages by her keeping a careful eye on what David and Steve had to say.

It is this unmatched combination of experience and
devotion that lie behind the information and advice in this
book. The same experience and devotion are the
foundation for the successes you can see on the television
screen and (better still) in the show ring.

You cannot learn to ride solely from a book, but you can
gain at least a glimpse of the *understanding* of the
relationship between horse and rider that is the key to all
the pleasure and all the success awaiting you in the years
ahead.

Welcome to the world of the horse

You have a powerful interest in horses. You want to learn to ride. You're not sure of the best way to go about it, so you have very sensibly decided to get the knowledge before you get the horse. You're exactly the person for whom we've written this book.

Your very first step, and certainly the best one, is to meet a few horses face to face. See if you like them. See if they like you. For the most part, horses are friendly, intelligent, inquisitive creatures – individuals, with individual personalities. You'll find that making friends with horses is just like making friends with people: it takes time. So don't rush it.

Now for this book. The first part concentrates on the basic techniques used to establish the rider comfortably in the saddle. This comes before the section on ownership, because you can and should learn to ride on other people's horses before you get one of your own.

The second part of the book takes a look at all the new responsibilities involved when you not only ride but also become the owner of a horse. That horse is going to work very hard for you, so you must be prepared to work very hard for your horse.

We intend this book to be very practical. You can't learn to ride from a book, but you can gain the basic *understanding* you'll need when you're actually in charge of a horse. The book is fully and clearly illustrated, and there are wide margins so that you can make your own notes. The clear type makes quick reference easy, even in a stable's dim light on a dark winter evening.

So enjoy the book . . . enjoy learning to ride . . . and welcome to the world of the horse!

David Broome and Steve Hadley
June 1984

Part One **Ride**

You can start today

In a way, you *are* starting today – because you're reading our book! But that's not all you can do.

You can get in touch with the British Horse Society (National Equestrian Centre, Stoneleigh, Warwickshire) for the addresses of riding schools in your area that have been approved by the Society. This is very important. It's the best way to make sure that you enjoy the very highest standards of instruction, and the most conscientious concern for your safety. If you join a BHS-approved school, you can be confident that you, the instructors and the horses are all getting a square deal.

Secondly, you can get your body ready for riding without actually bothering a horse. How you set about this depends partly on your age. A young novice rider will not find much difficulty in adapting to the demands that riding makes upon the muscles; an older novice may have to face a period of suffering! There are three things the older novice can do. First, try a few gentle rides, and thus make sure that you do want to take it up seriously, justifying the extra effort to get fit. Secondly, regular riding can be supplemented by gentle exercises on the ground. In the house you can run up and down stairs; in the garden you can skip; and out on the road you can cycle. Thirdly, keep an eye on the advertisements for bath salts guaranteed to reduce muscular stiffness!

There is a third factor that's worth considering. Learning to ride (whether or not you get as far as owning a horse) involves a far from trivial outlay in time, effort and money. If and when you own a horse, you have to undertake a great deal of very hard work, and you must be prepared to let the welfare of your horse become a major responsibility in your life. Have you got what it takes? Now is the time to change your mind if you think you're not up to it.

Read the book, anyway. See if it will open the door to a whole new world of pleasure and satisfaction, where many new friends – people as well as horses – are waiting to welcome you.

The first exercises

'The seat . . . is the only thing that makes a horse go perfectly' – these words were written more than three hundred years ago, and they're just as true today.

The word 'seat' does not here refer to the rider's bottom. Nor, when you compliment a rider on 'a good seat', do you merely mean that his appearance is graceful and attractive. It refers to the *total physical relationship* between horse and rider, conveyed as it is through the contact of seat, legs and hands (through the reins).

Good hands, of course, are largely dependent on a good seat because the two are inter-related. To have good, independent hands, a rider must have a secure seat so that the hands are not used as a means of staying on board. However, there are always exceptions to the rule and because a rider has achieved a good, secure seat it does not necessarily follow that he will have good hands. He may simply be too ham-fisted to coordinate well.

As you will see when you read on, it is through physical contact that the rider communicates thoughts, instructions and even feelings, to make 'the horse go perfectly'.

You cannot, obviously, develop a good seat without the help of a horse, but you *can* start today, as promised. You can start experimenting with some exercises, and you can also acquire a bit of preliminary knowledge – an understanding of three words you will hear a lot in your first days at the riding school.

Balance refers to the muscular harmony between horse and rider. That is to say, it's more than just not falling off. Every horse moves differently, and the experienced rider is immediately and instinctively responsive to the individual pattern of movement.

Impulsion is a little difficult to define because it has two aspects, rather like the word 'acceleration' in motoring. There is the latent energy in the horse's muscles (or the car's engine), and there is the rider's (or driver's) power to put that energy to work through the controlling communication – muscular contact if it's a horse, and a touch on the accelerator if it's a car.

Control means exactly what it says: the rider is in control of the horse, deciding when to start and when to stop, what pace to use (walk, trot, canter or gallop), whether to turn right or left, and so on. Specific methods of exercising control are usually referred to as **aids**.

Aids fall into two distinct categories: the *natural* and the *artificial*. The natural aids are applied by the legs, hands, voice and heels. A good, obedient – that is to say, well-trained – horse will respond to these aids in a relaxed, easy manner if they are used correctly. However, should the horse be unwilling or reluctant to cooperate, or, indeed, slow to react, he needs to be quickened up by the use of artificial aids – whip and spurs. But before the new rider starts to prod or hit the horse, it's as well for him to question his own ability to apply the natural aids. The horse may well not be to blame and by using those artificial aids, he will simply become confused and truculent. So, make sure that you know exactly what you are doing before you blame the animal.

The three technical terms highlight three aspects of communication between horse and rider. The next time you're at a horse show, visit the practice ring and pick out a rider who has an unmistakably 'good seat'. You may, at this moment, wonder how you will recognise it; but you'll find, when you get there, that it really *is* unmistakable. The rider with a 'good seat' is, above all, *relaxed*. He or she looks perfectly at home in the saddle, without any of the stiffness or mechanical movement that will, inevitably, communicate itself to the horse.

When you look at such a rider, you'll find that you can say to yourself: 'Ah yes! I *see* what balance means. I can *see* impulsion at work. I can *see* the rider exercising control.' It should remind you of the mythical centaur – the body of a horse controlled by the mind of a man. That is close to what you yourself will be aiming at if you decide to become a serious rider; it will be a marvellous and unmistakable experience when, for the very first time, you achieve this unison of will and movement.

It's time to remind ourselves that, in between the body of the horse and the mind of the man, there is also the body of the man (or woman) to be considered. It's going to work harder than usual, and it is also going to use some muscles that may have been allowed to get somewhat lazy in most people's daily round in home, school or office.

First, give your body the sort of exercise that anyone can enjoy – jogging, skipping, even just running up and down stairs. That will do you good anyway and will tone up the muscles if you want to do more.

Next, there are some basic exercises that are specifically designed to prepare you for the saddle (see photographs). If you're serious about riding, you will be well advised to do these exercises every day; but develop the routines gradually . . . exercise gently rather than over-vigorously . . . always break off before you get too tired.

Exercises to help you achieve the feel of the back-muscle action you will need when riding. Standing in front of a table with a book protruding over its edge, you can push the book onto the table without using your hands just by bracing your back.

Similarly, you can tilt a shooting stick (or stool) by the same action. Always be careful not to hollow your back.

Remember that the purpose of these exercises is to make you more *aware* of the muscles involved in developing a good seat – *not* to make them stronger. You need not be beefy to be a good rider, but you do have to develop more than ordinary sensitivity to pressure and movement.

As far as the legs are concerned, you would do well to start exercising as soon as possible, because these *are* strengthening exercises, and – if riding is going to be your major interest in life – there's a long way to go. If, on the other hand, it is to be a pleasure rather than a serious, exacting and competitive sport, you can treat your poor old muscles a good deal more gently, though at any level there's a great deal of pleasure to be found in taking the job seriously. You don't need apparatus at all if you can embark on a regular programme of jogging, running on the spot, knees-bend exercises and the like. In any case, the most effective piece of apparatus is the ordinary bicycle. The professional jockey would set himself a two-week programme, starting with easy rides for fifteen minutes a day and building up gradually to a daily forty-five minutes of *hard* riding. As you are not a professional jockey (yet), you can scale this down to a routine that is rather less exacting and a good deal more pleasurable. Always remember that no useful purpose can possibly be served by exhausting yourself.

A last word: although these are preliminary exercises for use before you start riding, they will still be valuable later on as a supplement to exercises performed when you are actually in the saddle. They're particularly good for the *wind* – you'll be surprised to find how out of breath you get when you thought it was the horse that was doing all the work!

What to wear

There's one thing about riding that everybody knows – even the layman who doesn't know the difference between a crupper and a curry comb: the rider has to wear a hard hat.

That's absolutely right. It's the one article of riding

clothing which we consider to be compulsory. Never, never ride without your hard hat. Everybody falls off a horse sooner or later. We have (not often recently – but now and again!). It's the well-fitting hard hat that can save riders from possible serious injury. It will do the same for you if you remember to wear it when riding – *always*. But just any hat won't do and certainly not a second-hand item which may have been damaged before it came to you. There's absolutely no point in having a hat on your head if, as soon as you fall off the horse, the hat falls off with you. Make sure that, at the very least, the hat fits well. Here's a good method to check on how well the hat fits. Once you've got it on your head, tap the peak firmly. If it hits you on the nose or falls off altogether, then it obviously isn't going to stay on your head very long once you are on the horse. A sensible precaution adopted by many riders nowadays is also to use a safety harness to hold the hat properly in place.

Hats can, of course, be made-to-measure. They will be a lot more expensive but the price of your safety cannot be too great. And, sadly, head injuries are all too common.

Finally, don't forget that if you damage your own hat, throw it away and get a new one.

Apart from a hard hat, you have considerable freedom of choice in clothing. You do *not* have to invest in a complete kit of costly clothes – especially at the outset, when you cannot possibly tell whether riding is going to be a life-long passion or an undemanding, irregular hobby. It is, though, a necessary courtesy to be as neatly turned out as your fellow riders and your instructors – and the horse. It's plain common sense to be comfortable. And you do have to give special consideration to *safety*.

Shoes, for example, can be a death-trap. Sandals can fall off . . . half-soles can catch in the stirrups . . . high heels and studs are both dangerous. You need shoes with a medium heel and a through-sole, or proper jodphur boots. Rubber riding boots are also ideal. They're not expensive; they look good; and they're easily wiped clean after a muddy ride.

A long trailing scarf is a particularly stupid thing to wear when riding. Just think of all the things the free end can

Sarah shows a good position in the saddle and she and her pony are a fine example of a well turned out pair.

get caught in when the other end is firmly wrapped round your neck. Leave it behind.

Coloured jodphurs look good and don't show the dirt as much as the traditional beige ones, but neat jeans or cords are acceptable and the stretch variety are particularly useful for casual riding.

Wear the sweaters, jackets or anoraks you already have. Protect your calves and knees from sore patches by thick socks or woolly tights. Wear gloves not only for warmth but to protect your hands from blisters. Enlarge your wardrobe as you need to do so, and as you can spare the money. When you graduate to competitions, you will have to appear in the correct formal wear, but it is not strictly necessary in the earlier stages of learning to ride.

Just one last note on tidiness in the saddle: if your hair is long, please tie it back or wear a hair-net. Long hair escaping from under a hard hat in every direction looks slovenly and can even be a minor safety hazard.

Where to go

Let us suppose that you have received a list of riding schools in your neighbourhood from the British Horse Society. Any one of them will give you first-class instruction. Apart from comparing fees, what can you do to make the right choice between them? You can go to see them.

There is certainly plenty of useful information you can get from a prospectus or in correspondence, but that is no substitute for using your own eyes and making your own judgement. Consider the most important questions, and notice that the only way of getting the answers is to go and *see* for yourself.

At each of the schools you visit, look around and ask yourself: is the stable yard clean? Are the boxes sturdy, clean and draught-proof? Are the horses in good condition? Are their coats well groomed and gleaming? Are their eyes bright and inquisitive?

Pleasant looking stables with alert and inquisitive horses. Note the safety precautions of a fire bucket and extinguisher and an outside safety light switch placed well away from where the horse could reach it.

A happy relationship with your friend, the horse, is very important – but not more important than the relationship with your friend, the instructor. Will you get on well with the people who will be teaching you? Can you see in them the same enthusiasm for teaching that you have for learning? Can you be sure that running a riding school is, for them, more than just a way of earning a living?

Let us suppose that you've confidently picked the best available riding school in your district. You've made up your mind to work very hard, to take aching muscles and the occasional hard knock in your stride. You're going to persevere until you really feel at home in the world of the horse. Is there any single piece of advice we can give you that, more than any other, will help you to success?

Yes – *don't be afraid to ask questions!*

We've already stressed the need to *understand* what you're doing, and why, when you learn to ride. That means that you *will* have to ask questions sometimes. Asking a

David and his young pupil obviously have a happy relationship. (Note, incidentally, the safety stirrups, the outer side of which, made of rubber, will come off if the child has a fall and thus insure that his foot is not caught in the stirrup. See whether your prospective riding school employs this safety precaution for young children.)

question does not mean that you, the pupil, are ignorant, or stupid, or slow on the uptake. It can mean that the instructor has used a technical term without previously explaining it to you – of course you won't understand! He might give you a piece of information without realising that, unless explained, it doesn't make much sense. For example, he may say: 'Toes up, heels down.' You, the obedient pupil, try to remember to do what you're told, but without knowing what it is that you're trying to achieve. Ask the question, and you'll learn that this is to keep the leg long and around the horse, and to bring the heel into the best position to create forward movement. Simple, isn't it?

An enthusiastic instructor will never mind answering your questions, and you, in your turn, must not mind asking them. It is, however, possible that you may have an instructor who is *not* an enthusiast – impatient, perhaps, at being asked to explain what he means. This just could be a clue to the discovery that you're at the wrong riding school. If so, don't stay. You owe it to yourself to learn with the best teachers; and you owe it to the horses you are going to ride to make the best possible start.

Let's suppose you've solved this problem . . . picked a good school . . . struck lucky with your instructor . . . and are just going to meet the horse. We'll assume that you've struck lucky with the horse too. He's a lot bigger and stronger than you are, but he'll be tolerant and good-tempered. When a novice rider gets confused, does things wrong, gives the horse signals he doesn't understand, he will remain calm and good-tempered, leaving it to the instructor to sort things out. So what's ahead of you in your first riding lesson?

Before you read on, don't forget that different schools and different instructors vary greatly in their methods. They may explain things differently, or arrange their lessons in a different order. Don't let it worry you if other people's instruction varies in detail from the lessons we would give you if we could meet you personally. Read the book to gain understanding and confidence, and then trust the instructor – and, of course, the horse!

Mounting

Of course, before you mount the horse, he has got to be
tacked up. Now, in ninety-nine cases out of a hundred, the
riding school you've chosen will have your horse ready for
you. But, just occasionally, something may go wrong and
you may be asked to tack up the horse yourself. It's not a
particularly complicated job when you know what you're
doing and, after a little practice, you will find it perfectly
simple, but it's not a job to take on before your first lesson.
Ask for the horse to be tacked up for you and, quite a bit
later on, learn to do the job yourself. Now you're ready to
meet the horse.

You're going to be in charge of this rather large animal.
You're going to tell him what to do. You're also going to see
that he does do what you tell him to do. And first of all you
have to get up there. It won't be at all surprising if you find
that you're a bit nervous. The big disadvantage here is that
your nervousness may make the horse nervous too; and the
result may be only too accurately described as 'getting off
to a bad start'.

So let us see what help it could be to achieve that
preliminary *understanding* that we keep stressing.
Consider this very first task from the horse's point of view.

You're a stranger. If you put your weight on one of the
stirrups in order to mount, you tug the saddle sideways,
which is very uncomfortable for the horse. You heave
yourself into the air and land with a thud in the saddle.
The horse doesn't care for a wallop in the middle of his
back any more than you would if you were in his place. Can
you make a better start to the partnership between you and
the horse?

Yes. You can introduce yourself, so that you're not quite
a stranger. You start where he can see you on his near side
(his left – same as a car) and walk confidently towards him
on a straight line between his shoulder and head, talking as
you go. He won't understand what you're saying to him,
but he will respond to your voice. Talk confidently . . . offer
friendship . . . and you'll plant the seed of mutual
understanding on which the whole relationship depends.

Touching is also important. Pat the horse's neck and

body. Stroke his face and muzzle – do *not* pat it. You would not want people to bang your face, however affectionately, and the horse doesn't like it either. Do *not* try to ingratiate yourself with a horse by blowing up his nose. We can't positively say this doesn't work. The technique has attracted a vast amount of publicity and, for certain people, it may very well do the trick. But we're concerned with the danger you put yourself in if you start a relationship with a horse in this fashion. He's got a big mouth, full of powerful teeth, so please do think about it.

Another mistake is giving the horse lumps of sugar or other titbits. These can be given when a reward is due, and *only* then; but don't use them to bribe your way into the horse's good books, because that just gets you both into bad habits.

So the introductions are over. Put your left arm through the reins in order to stop the horse walking off while you check that the girth is reasonably tight (just room for two fingers in between horse and girth) and make sure that both stirrup leathers are pulled down.

This is the point at which you take charge. You want the horse to stand still so that you can mount. If he wants to move off, you mustn't let him. So you have to establish control immediately.

You cannot, while you are standing on the ground, control the horse by physical contact through seat or legs; so you have to use your hands – or, rather, the contact between your hands and the horse's mouth provided by the reins. This is how it's done: you hold the reins loosely in the left hand, resting that hand on the horse's withers; then use the right hand to draw the reins through the left, and make sure that they are evenly in contact with the horse's mouth. A light and gentle touch is quite enough to signal to the horse that you are in charge. Always remember that the horse's mouth is very sensitive indeed, and you must treat it delicately. This is partly to avoid hurting the horse, but also to encourage the sensitivity of communication between the horse and you which, as we explained, is the key to riding success.

Use your right hand to hold the near-side stirrup iron, and put your left foot firmly in it. Take the back of the

Standing by the horse's shoulder and facing the rear, take the reins in the left hand at the horse's withers;

Take the back of the stirrup and turn it towards you, placing your left foot in it;

Hop round to face the saddle;

Put your right hand flat on the saddle and spring up;

Swing your right leg over, keeping well clear of the horse's hindquarters.

Holding the reins correctly. (For the sake of clarity, the loose ends are down the horse's right shoulder.)

stirrup and turn it towards you (the picture shows how) so that when you are mounted the leathers are not twisted and rubbing against your shin or boot. Place the right hand flat on top of the saddle. It is put there purely for balance. Do *not* clutch the saddle – do *not* haul yourself up by sheer muscle! You *spring* into the saddle, rather than climbing into it.

If you are very short and the horse is very tall, you may need a mounting block of some kind to make this movement feasible. You have to spring far enough into the air to be able to swing that right leg over the horse's back, and, with an effortless flowing movement, land gently in the saddle. Make sure you don't kick the horse in the ribs with your left toe. Don't kick his hindquarters with your right foot and don't, as you are springing up, take your left hand off the horse's withers and use the reins to balance yourself or you will give the horse a nasty jab in the mouth. Don't flop into the saddle with your full weight. And, of course, don't be discouraged if you're not all that graceful at the first attempt.

Now you have to get your right foot into the off-side stirrup iron. Remember the rule that, when in the saddle, you don't look down. And that's common sense really. If your eyes are on the ground, you can't see where you are going. And furthermore, you can't see the obstacles or problems that the horse can see. And that, of course, also applies when you have the animal at a halt. Share with him everything that's in his view so that should something appear which might frighten him, you'll be immediately aware of it. Now to follow that rule certainly requires a bit of practice but you should soon be able to get your foot in the other stirrup while still sitting relaxed and erect.

Now make sure that you are holding the reins correctly. They go over the little finger (and, obviously, below the ring finger), up across the palms, over the forefinger with the thumb lying along the reins. The loose ends fall down the horse's shoulder inside the left rein to avoid putting extra weight on the horse's mouth. The only exception is that, if you are carrying a whip in the left hand, the reins fall down the right shoulder to avoid the risk of getting entangled with the whip.

27

It takes a long time to describe, but it's a very quick process – once you've learned how to do it right. It is very important that the horse should not be allowed to move off until you give the signal. This encourages good manners and reduces the chances of an accident.

Before we deal with moving off in detail, we should mention two other ways of mounting the horse, both easier than the method already described as long as they are carried out with a degree of confidence. The first is the leg-up (the system used by trainers to help jockeys up before a race). It's perhaps the quickest way of mounting and a competent person can help a whole string of riders up in a very short time. But do not count on the helping hand; it is simple common sense to be independent of all help. Suppose you come off in the middle of a field miles from home. You either mount by yourself or walk the horse home. Better to mount, eh?

Now, here is the leg-up procedure. Face square on to the saddle; take the reins in the left hand and throw the loose ends over the horse's right shoulder; grasp the withers firmly with the left hand (still holding the reins); put the right hand on the back of the saddle; bend the left leg. The trainer, groom, instructor or other helper now puts his hands under the knee and ankle of your bent left leg and hoists you into the air as you spring with the right leg. This minimises the drag on the saddle through the left stirrup and also ensures that you land lightly in the saddle. In other words, it's easier on the horse as well as easier for you. Practise giving as well as receiving the leg-up, because you'll be expected to help friends and fellow-learners.

The easiest of all methods is the mounting block – by which you just climb onto the horse. Many purpose-built mounting blocks survive from past centuries, a couple of stone steps about 75cm high built near the village church or town hall so that aged rectors and plump aldermen could clamber onto their horses and ride home from work. A gate, a grass bank, a tree stump or the bumper of a Land Rover can also do duty as a mounting block. There is nothing wrong with using any of these – it's the easiest method of all for the horse as well as for you.

Ready for off?

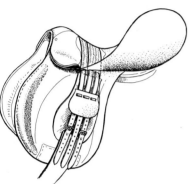

Make a final check of the girth, because your weight in the saddle will have slackened it and it will almost certainly need tightening by at least one hole. Put your left leg forward; raise the saddle flap; take hold of the first girth strap and tighten it, and then the second (do *not* loosen both straps at the same time in case the saddle slips round and you fall off). Then run your hand between the girth and the horse's side to make sure you haven't pinched a bit of his flesh.

While we're talking about the girth, there's a point of safety to remember. You'll find three straps attached to the saddle to secure the girth, two of which are sewn onto one piece of webbing and the third onto another. Obviously if you use both the straps on the double piece, and the stitching breaks, then you and the saddle come off. The safe method is to buckle one onto the double and the other onto the single strap. That may sound complicated, but a look at the saddle will show you exactly what we mean.

Check the length of the stirrup leathers, making sure they are the same. Length is a matter for individual preference, but the novice will find it safer to have them a little too short rather than a little too long. There are two rough guides to the correct length: when you're standing on the ground with your arm outstretched and the finger-tips just touching the buckle on the stirrup leather, the tread of the stirrup iron should just reach your armpit; when in the saddle with your leg hanging loose and your foot out of the stirrup iron, the tread should just touch your ankle.

(Incidentally, it is a good thing to familiarise yourself with the correct way to tack up and untack the horse – not merely to confine your interest to these essential checks. We deal with this in more detail on later pages when we discuss your responsibility as the horse's owner.)

Now you are ready for the last moments of preparation before moving off . . .

Posture correct, with your weight firmly in the middle of the saddle, shoulders squared but not stiff, sitting upright but relaxed, with head up and eyes looking ahead and legs resting naturally against the horse's sides. Hands holding the reins slightly in front of and above the pommel of the saddle, gently controlling the horse by the light touch on his mouth. Knee and toe turned slightly away so that heel and lower calf are kept constantly in contact with the horse's sides. Head, shoulders, hips and heels all in a vertical straight line. Arms relaxed and hands about four inches apart.

'From the heel to the hand.'

Remember the phrase – it handily sums up the whole process of controlling the horse when he starts to move off. The legs provide the impulsion, getting the horse to start moving or to change gait; the hands convey messages to the moving horse, to change his direction, for example. If you're a motorist, the analogy with the car will strike you at once. Foot on the accelerator applies the engine's energy; hands on the steering wheel control and guide the moving car.

So, at last, we come to the moment to which all this talk has been leading . . .

Moving off

Three more technical terms: as you will see, they refer to three distinct stages in moving your horse off, but they blend, in practice, into a single instinctive process.

Position means just what it says. It means that the rider is in the correct posture already described, upper arms vertical and relaxed, forearms making a straight line with the reins from elbows to horse's mouth.

Collection is also almost self-explanatory: the rider 'collects' the horse together. Gentle contact through the reins on the mouth and gentle contact with the heels on the horse's sides prompt mental alertness and physical readiness.

Preparation is the final stage before actually moving off. The rider has a clear and confident intention, and transmits it to the horse so that he knows exactly what he has to do.

Think for a moment of that word 'intention'. It's the key to what may, at first, seem the difficult and mysterious business of controlling the horse. Imagine that you're going to catch a bus, and it arrives at the bus stop when you are still some distance away. If you think that you can get to the bus before it leaves the stop, you *form an intention* to catch it. Your brain doesn't think of this as a task needing specific instructions to left foot, then right foot, then left, then right. It doesn't even transmit the command 'Run!'. As soon as you *form the intention* to catch the bus, every part of your physical machinery automatically performs its own bit of the total task – even including the involuntary muscles that quicken your breathing and heart-beat.

This can even operate on another person. When two expert ballroom dancers take the floor, the one who leads will form a whole series of intentions. Each one will be accurately followed by the partner just as though they had rehearsed them together – even if they have just met for the first time. Each knows what is expected by the other, and the purely mental intention is subtly transmitted by almost imperceptible pressures, movements and even facial expressions. This is very close to what happens when you *form an intention* to move off on your horse.

You and the horse do, of course, have to learn the physical 'code' through which the intention in your head travels the subtle path to the horse's legs. And there are techniques to be practised. But all this will be wasted unless you, the rider, can form a clear, concise and confident intention in your own mind; and then convey it

Here David has collected his horse in readiness to move off in walk.

with authority. If you are confused, the horse will be confused. If the intention is crystal clear in your own mind, it becomes possible for the horse to respond with smooth, prompt and instinctive obedience to your instruction.

When you move off, it will naturally be at a walking pace. This is the first of the four quite different paces (or gaits) at which you can ride.

The paces or gaits

The walk contains four steps to each stride. That is to say, the horse moves one leg at a time. When you form the intention to walk, you close your heels round the horse and lightly squeeze with heels and lower leg. The horse should start to walk. If he doesn't, prompt him by a short, sharp tap with your heels. Maintain a light contact with the horse's mouth, allowing his head freedom of movement. Common sense will tell you that you must *continue* to convey your intention to the horse if you want him to continue walking. Keep up the impulsion.

THE WALK

THE TROT

The trot is obviously faster than the walk, but it is also a different kind of gait. There are two steps to a stride instead of four. The horse's diagonal *pairs* of legs move alternately, near fore and off hind followed by off fore and near hind; these are called, respectively, left diagonal and right diagonal.

This makes a bumpy ride, the rider being bounced out of the saddle and dropped back into it again. The problem is very simply solved if the rider rises and sits in the same rhythm as that of the horse. Put your weight into the stirrups, keeping the heels down. But don't run away with the idea that it's going to be easy. Achieving a balance with the rising trot is just about the most difficult thing that the new rider has to learn. From the outset, everything seems out of balance. You'll slip from side to side and feel as though you're falling off, and you quite possibly will, at some point in the early lessons, take a tumble. Now it's here, at the very beginning of your riding life, that bad habits can be formed. *Do not grip with the knees*. Imagine your legs as creating a 'frame' around the horse. For the rising movement, use the whole leg and for the return

33

sitting movement let the knee simply control the way the body returns to the saddle. A relaxed ease of movement is necessary in both the rising and the sitting part of the trot. Eventually you'll find that the heels and knees are used to control and maintain the balance of your body on the horse, but at no point do you grip with either knee or heel.

The early lessons will be very much concerned with establishing the seat. And, during these lessons, you will probably be asked to ride without stirrups and to endeavour to rise without stirrup aid. We do accept that this exercise technique will help an unsure rider to gain more initial confidence and balance but, in so doing, the novice rider will be gripping with the leg, and if this habit sticks, there's no chance of that 'frame' we talked about becoming part of the riding style. Nor will the relaxed ease of movement we're so intent on you achieving be possible. However, here's a seat-establishing exercise which we thoroughly recommend. When sitting on your horse with *no stirrups,* move both legs together away from the horse's sides in an upwards then outwards movement from the hip. Try to do this without altering your seat position on the saddle, though you may hold on to the front of the saddle to control your balance. Endeavour to maintain a straight back all the time. Ride regularly without stirrups because it opens the seat bones, allows you to sit deeper in the saddle and finally, and most importantly during the early days, removes any stiffness.

When you've achieved a reasonable degree of confidence and balance in the rising trot, you'll hear your instructor calling for you to be on the **correct diagonal.** If you haven't heard this phrase before, you are likely to find it rather confusing. The movement of the horse's shoulders provides the complete answer for you. Suppose you are riding a left-handed circle or bend. Now glance down at the horse's outside (right) shoulder. It's obviously moving up and down in rhythm. When you have established that you are rising as the horse's right shoulder goes forward, then you are on the correct diagonal. It obviously follows that when you are riding a right-hand circle or bend, you are looking to the horse's left shoulder to give you the point of rise. The immediate comfort and superior balance you

This exercise will aid balance and help the legs to move independently from the upper body without destroying the elegant position already achieved.

achieve will be obvious. Less obvious, but more necessary, is your understanding of how the horse reacts physically to your use of diagonals. If, for instance, you continue to exercise your horse on the left rein, then his muscles can become one-sided. It should be clear to you that, on a continued left-handed or right-handed movement, one set of muscles will take a greater strain than the other. Make absolutely sure, therefore, that you change rein and therefore diagonals very frequently to avoid stiffness in the horse.

The object is also, and importantly, that the rider's weight is completely in the saddle as the horse's inside hind leg is on the ground. The horse remains in balance and you will have a driving influence on that leg to move it upwards and forwards. It's vital with your understanding of the trotting seat to avoid getting either behind or in front of the horse's movement. Endeavour to keep your inside leg (that's your left if you are on the left rein) beneath you with the heel in line with the hip and the knee slightly away from the saddle. The outside leg should be slightly behind the girth and lightly laid on the side of the horse. While riding the circle, make sure you resist the natural tendency to bend, rather 'follow' the circle with your shoulders.

Make sure you always land softly back into the saddle and let the knee aid you in the lowering process – there should be no sound at all as your seat arrives on the saddle. Make sure also that you don't use your hands to pull yourself up into the rise. Obviously this would be extremely uncomfortable for the horse and would only underline the fact that your seat in the rising trot was not established. Check and check again your lower leg position. This controls the balance of the top of the body. If the lower leg moves, the body will be badly balanced.

There is also the sitting trot, which allows you to make the transition from trot to walk or trot to canter.

The canter is a more complicated gait with three beats to a stride. In a 'left canter', the horse first moves his off hind leg; then the right diagonal (off fore and near hind

35

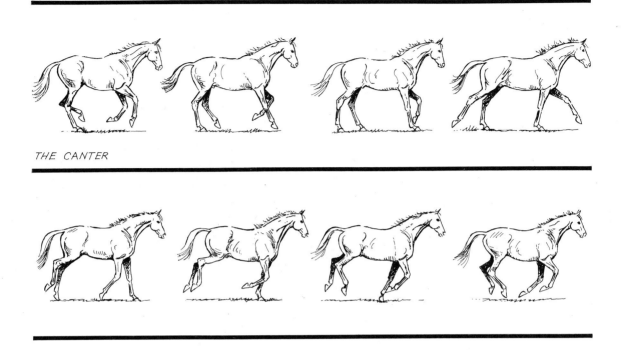

THE CANTER

together); finally the near fore. Then the sequence is repeated. The 'right canter' is obviously the opposite: near hind, left diagonal, off fore.

As the horse will most easily strike off into a canter on a bend or corner, imagine that you are in a sitting trot and approaching a left-hand bend. You *form the intention* to canter. This means that you will sit more firmly in the saddle, slightly shorten the left rein, maintaining contact with the outside rein, and increase the pressure with your legs. There is now a slight difference in the position of the legs. Your left leg is on the girth, but the right leg is slightly behind it – aiming, as it were, at the off hind leg to start the left canter sequence. If the horse fails to pick up the canter within a few strides, don't try to force him. Collect him by taking checks with each rein alternately, at the same time sitting deep in the saddle to slow him down and re-balance him. Keep the lower legs close against his sides to stop him drifting off course. Then, when the horse is going steadily again, try again with clear, definite aids at the next convenient corner.

Needless to say, if you were going into a right-hand bend, you would do exactly the same except for reading 'left' instead of 'right' and vice versa throughout.

The seat at canter should be elegant and relaxed. Remember to keep your legs long and relaxed at all times, for in your early riding days you'll find that your legs have a tendency to draw up and grip too much. The end result of this habit will be loss of balance, then stirrups, then seat. Nevertheless, the canter is the most comfortable of all gaits if you remember two more things: first, *sit still,* going with the rocking-horse motion; second, maintain the impulsion or forward movement.

The gallop is a pace that should not (if all goes well) concern the novice rider at all. You should not risk a gallop until you have enough experience to be sure you can control a powerful – and, perhaps, wilful – horse at his fastest pace.

'But,' you may ask, 'suppose the horse gallops anyway?'

It's true that horses do occasionally run away with their riders, and you ought to know what to do.

THE GALLOP

For a start, you keep calm and quiet. You hang on to the idea that you're the boss. If the horse has formed his own intention to gallop, you form an opposing intention that he shall slow down. Then decide how to ensure that your intention is the one that will win. It depends where you are. If you're in a field and a horse runs away with you, turn him into a circle, making that circle smaller and smaller until it becomes increasingly difficult for the horse to gallop and easier for the rider to regain control.

If you're riding in a track or lane, stay aboard if you can. Look for something at which to aim the horse, but be sure it's high enough and solid enough to stop him jumping it. Fortunately, most horses eventually pull themselves up without doing any damage. If not, it's up to you to pull him up, and there are two ways to do it.

First, you can sit down in the saddle with plenty of weight in the stirrups so that your seat is secure, and then square your shoulders. Don't be tempted to stand in the stirrups and haul back on the reins. That position makes it impossible to use your back action. Keep taking several hard checks with a give-and-take action. This give-and-take action is necessary because using one long desperate pull will only have the effect of making the horse pull back at you – a battle in which you have no chance of being the victor.

The second method is to crouch forward, shortening the reins and using the same give-and-take action, and treating the horse to a few soothing (and forgiving) words.

That's the technique of the emergency stop, but what about more normal occasions?

Halting and dismounting

Stopping is easy. You have been 'thinking forward' all the time the horse has been moving in order to keep him going at the correct pace. As soon as you 'think rest' and allow the thought to travel through back, seat and legs, the horse will sense this as an instruction to halt. He will feel your weight heavier in the saddle and realise that *your* legs are no longer urging on *his* legs. This technique applies when riding a quiet, docile, or even reluctant animal, but the system changes with a more active horse.

In such a case you will have to concentrate on getting him to stop. Square the shoulders and firm the back. Sit deep in the saddle with legs long and around the horse, your weight well into the heel. Do not allow the lower leg to go forward. With the hands, produce a series of give-and-take movements, much like squeezing a sponge. These, together with the seat and leg aids, should bring the horse to a halt in a nice balanced fashion. The same principle is applied when moving to a slower pace. This is called a 'downward transition'. Once you have achieved a steady halt, you can dismount. Take both reins in the left hand (and the whip, if you have one). Rest your left hand lightly on the horse's withers and your right on the pommel of the saddle. Remove both feet from the stirrups. Lean slightly forward. Swing your right leg up and over the horse's hindquarters and, with a vaulting action, turn the body,

Left hand holding the reins on the horse's withers, right on the pommel and both feet out of the stirrups;

Push up and swing your right leg over, being careful not to hit the horse's hindquarters;

Push slightly away from the horse . . .

And land lightly on the ground.

push slightly away from the horse and land lightly on the toes facing the saddle. Take the reins over the horse's head and loop them over the left arm; run the stirrups up the leathers; loosen the girth a couple of holes (not more, in case the saddle slips). Lead the horse away, facing forwards and walking by his shoulder on his left side – do *not* pull him. Your right hand is now holding the reins just below the bit with your left hand near the buckle to keep the reins safely off the ground and away from the horse's front legs. It's not an uncommon sight, particularly in Western films, to see a rider dismount by swinging the right leg over the horse's neck and sliding off. *This is highly dangerous.* It can startle the horse at the same time as you

Never dismount this way. You can see how dangerous it would be if the horse threw its head up or moved forward suddenly, and how Steve has no control over it as he dismounts.

abandon control of him; and, if he shies away sharply, you can land with a crash on your back. Many riders have been seriously injured by dismounting this way.

Where do you go from here?

We hope you go from this book to a good riding school endorsed by the BHS. Whatever your ambition (riding as part of your profession, competitive riding or just riding for pleasure), the very first steps will be much the same, and you might like a brief sketch of what will be ahead of you.

Your first course of lessons can be just as long as you wish – and need. You may learn quickly or slowly; you may have much time to spare, or just an hour or so in any one week. Don't forget that top-class riders still seek advice and tuition despite all their experience; you never stop learning!

The very first lessons are simple and are devoted to getting you used to this unfamiliar world: tacking up, mounting, dismounting, simple exercises on horseback.

Children, needless to say, are looked after with especially great care. They ride safe, trustworthy ponies on a lead rein in the charge of a reliable assistant. Adult novices can have a similarly reassuring introduction by having their first lessons on a 'lunge'. This is a long lead rein with an instructor at one end and the horse at the other, the latter going round in a large circle under the control of the instructor at the centre.

Steve giving a lunge lesson in his indoor school.

This is a very positive method of establishing the novice rider, or indeed a more experienced rider, in the correct seat. It's a way of checking and re-checking your position on the horse and can be done in a number of different ways – no stirrups or reins, no reins, no reins and short stirrups – and allows the instructor, with control, to correct those early mistakes and re-establish in an experienced rider things which may have gone wrong.

For variety, novices may be taken for a hack or road ride. This is a good way to emphasise the pleasure of riding without having to concentrate too hard on correcting faults and polishing technique.

When riding on the road, it is vital to remember that road safety is, if anything, even more important for horse and rider than for any other road user. Failures of courtesy as well as caution can have disastrous results. Always ride on the left in Britain. Never ride more than two abreast. If riding with others, keep close together to make things as simple as possible for the overtaking motorist, who, if he is careful, considerate and understands the problems of horse and rider, will slow down. Should he do so, natural courtesy insists that you should thank him by raising a hand in acknowledgement or nodding your head. An inconsiderate motorist can be a serious hazard, and you will do well to set impeccable standards of courtesy, even if others are slow to follow your example. Keep off the pedestrians' footpaths, and *never* canter or gallop on the road. It's simply too dangerous from so many points of view. Your horse may slip on the hard, and for him, highly polished road surface. He may shy at some surprising object or sudden movement, and in a flash he's out of control. Even if none of these incidents happens when you're on the road, the canter or gallop will cause damage to the horse's legs. They were not designed to bang up and down on tarmac or concrete. The damage you will cause could be serious and lasting, *so don't do it.*

There's one point worth making about riding schools: in the normal course of events, you will have the chance of riding a number of different horses. This is all to the good; every horse is different, and it will increase your confidence as well as your skill if your experience is as varied as possible. On the other hand, you may find that you get on especially good terms with one particular horse. If so, it's worth asking if you can stay with that horse for a few lessons, as that may well be the way to make the quickest progress.

Jumping

We're both well aware that a book by us without a section on jumping might seem at the least rather odd. Nevertheless, we have no intention of trying to cram a lifetime's experience into a few pages. It would be quite stupid to ask you to jump before you can canter properly and our introduction to the business of riding correctly is all this book is about. When you've truly mastered the basics of the craft, then and only then will you be ready to start jumping. It's our plan to write a complete study of jumping taking the rider from the very early stages right up to international show jumping level. For the moment we'll simply concentrate on an attitude that we want you to share when you think about jumping horses.

The horse, with a man on his back, has been jumping for centuries, but an understanding of how he jumps has only been looked at carefully for less than a hundred years. Before that time everything was instinctive for both horse and rider and it was as much a matter of luck that the right horse met the right rider. Now our understanding of the subject is much more detailed. On his own, a horse will do most things naturally; he'll make his way up and down extremely steep hills; he'll swim and jump, but only if he needs to. With jumping it's as simple and as difficult as to make him want to jump for *pleasure.* And in a nutshell that's why we don't want you jumping before you're totally relaxed and competent with your basic riding style. A horse with a nervous or even frightened rider on his back is not going to perform properly. That said, there's no harm in you starting to understand what's going on inside a jumping horse's head.

We can both say with absolute certainty that of all the horses we've ridden over the years, no two have been alike. As with people, the horse has an enormous range of personality and character and it's our job to come to terms with that character to get the best out of him. He can be any one of the following: brave, cowardly, over-ambitious, lazy, hot-tempered, quiet, sluggish or even downright timid. Making best use of the fine qualities and counteracting the worst is of vital importance in your handling of the animal. Some will need gentle coaxing and encouragement, responding best to a kind voice and hand. Others will be better with a more positive treatment involving a degree of discipline and a commanding attitude. Some horses will immediately jump for the sheer love of it and others will take more time. Be patient and understanding with those and in the end the result may be just as rewarding.

Whatever the horse's character, one thing they all have in common is an outstanding memory and never more so than when they've made a serious mistake at a fence, taken a heavy fall and hurt themselves. Then the worth of the horse comes to the fore. Next time out the good horse understands the problem and takes rather more care with the job, finds a little more elevation and tucks his legs closer to his body. The bad horse may well lose his nerve altogether after such an incident.

If you regard a good jumping horse as a super athlete then you won't be far wide of the mark. Peak condition and performance can only be achieved after a great deal of grindingly hard work on the part of the horse (that's why he's got to love it) and a similar effort from the rider.

There can be no set pattern for training a horse to jump, for while the basics will be pretty identical, the variations in individual methods of schooling will change with each horse, the method, of course, being linked to the character of the animal and the style and knowledge of the rider.

The expressions you'll be most likely to hear around the show ring, or at a race meeting where horses are hurdling or chasing, are many and varied (and most are not printable), but two will help us to illustrate the way into a perfect jump: 'he's stood off' or 'he's under it', meaning that the jump has been attempted with the point of take-off too far from the fence or the take-off has been too close. The ideal jump produces a perfect arc with the obstacle being dead centre at the highest point of the arc . . . the drawing shows exactly what we mean. To achieve the perfect jumping arc, the *approach* is of absolute importance. Initially the confidence and determination to jump is transmitted to the horse by the rider's attitude. Nervousness, fear or indecision are transmitted to the horse with equal speed. Remember, we're now talking about jumping at it's most simple and ordinary stage, the sort of jumping that you will soon be doing.

With a series of obstacles set up in a paddock, the best jumping pace is the canter. Certainly, a horse will jump from the walk or trot, but when cantering, the animal is moving in the perfect rhythm to jump. Now depending on the early schooling habits the horse has acquired, the

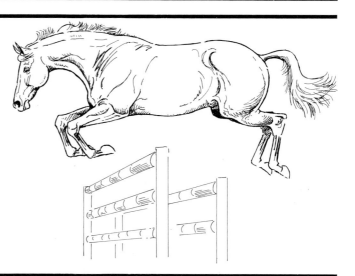

The ideal jump.

Here Tina demonstrates what happens when the horse gets too close in to the jump – she has been unable to pick up her front legs to get them over the pole. In show jumping, they will simply knock the pole down, but if they were riding across country over fixed fences, the consequences could be disastrous. Note, though, how still and well-balanced Tina is and how she is allowing the horse to stretch her neck forward to balance herself.

45

canter may be fast or slow. Some will get up a head of steam as the obstacle gets nearer while others will steady themselves and prepare with a degree of caution. But whichever situation you find yourself in, there's one golden rule to be obeyed:

SET THE HORSE ABSOLUTELY STRAIGHT AT THE JUMP.

When the point of take-off arrives, let him do the job himself. Pulling at the reins, raising the hands, tapping him with the whip or yelling won't help. The first three will only unbalance the animal, while a shout only encourages the rider, not the horse.

Once in the air, do not pull at his mouth, but ideally, keep in touch with it in the most gentle manner possible. The last thing a horse wants to feel, when he's in mid-air, is some idiot yanking at his mouth because they suddenly feel unsafe and frightened.

A good position over the jump – 'going with the horse'.

So what does happen for that fraction of time you're in the air? It all depends on the type of obstacle you're jumping. We all talk about 'going with the horse' and that expression should tell you clearly that if you're hanging on tight and leaning back – you're wrong! And that means in every sense. The balance you must find relies on your centre of gravity being ahead of that of the horse. Lean forward towards the horse's neck and keep your seat as much in touch with the saddle as possible. Through the jump your hands should be either side of the neck with the arms bent at the elbow to allow for a full stretch of the arm should that prove necessary. Gentle contact with the mouth throughout the jump requires skill and practice, and rather than exert that extra pressure, let your contact with the mouth go until you've landed. During the jump your horse must have the freedom to stretch his neck. This allows him to jump more freely and land with greater safety, since he uses his neck to balance himself.

As the jump is completed, the freedom the horse had in the air must be withdrawn on landing – second nature for the experienced rider, not necessarily so for the novice. When the front legs touch the ground, the rider's seat will still be out of the saddle and there it *must stay* until the back legs have touched down. Then the seat returns to the saddle and you gather up full control to start the next approach.

Throughout the approach and landing *never look down* and always look towards the next obstacle. You and the horse are going up and on – nothing must distract you from this object.

These are the very bare bones of the game, but if you drill them into your head before you start, life in the early stages will be much easier.

Sooner or later the key question will come up: should you have a horse of your own? There are obviously a number of conditions to be fulfilled before you can decide this: you'll need money, space for the horse, time and expert help close at hand. But none of these advantages will be of much use unless you have the necessary passion.

Read on, and see if we can help you to decide!

Part Two **A horse of your own?**

A horse of your own?

Many keen riders are prevented from owning horses for a number of reasons. Lack of money is the most obvious one. Lack of space can be another – you can't keep a horse in a suburban back garden. But lack of time may well be the most serious obstacle, and the one we want to emphasise here. A horse needs care and attention 365 days in the year and he has to have it whether his owner feels like it or not. If you live in the middle of a city, the time taken up travelling to your horse and home again may be a sizeable chunk of the day. So think very carefully. Does your life have room for a horse of your own?

You probably won't be able to answer this question without knowing a lot more about it. That's exactly why we've written the second part of this book. Suppose you can raise the money. Suppose you're sure you will have the time. Now read on . . .

Buying a horse

In the bad old days, men who dealt in second-hand horses had the kind of reputation that, today, is sometimes earned by men who deal in second-hand cars. A horse-coper was assumed to be a rogue, and, even now, 'horse-trading' is a slang term for bargaining of doubtful morality. We may be living in more honest times (or, of course, not!), but it is still possible to make bad mistakes. Guard against this by taking very seriously the advice we are going to give you.

First, ask yourself what you can expect from the people you are dealing with. If, for example, you are buying from a dealer, you can be certain that he wants to make a profit on the deal – quite rightly, of course. What you may not know (unless you've been able to make an unusually thorough investigation) is whether any given dealer is as concerned about customer-satisfaction as he is about profit.

You may decide that it is a lot safer to buy your first horse from a horse-owning friend. Here, we can only say that you have to be careful about friends too. We are not suggesting that any friend of yours would knowingly entice you into a bad bargain; but, when novice horse-buyer meets amateur horse-dealer, it is only too easy for both parties to end up regretting the deal.

The way out of this problem is simple, and it is our second important point: never buy a horse without the help and advice of someone more expert than yourself.

The person who taught you to ride will certainly know far better than you the sort of horse that's going to be suitable. There's clearly no point in buying a horse that's used to hunting twice a week when your abilities stretch only to three hours' simple hacking. Another source of advice might well come from an experienced friend who will know better the type of conditions that you can afford in terms of looking after the animal and therefore save you from buying a horse used to four-star treatment when the best you can do is two-star. Now, having chosen your horse, before you settle on buying him, there's one further, and vital, step to take. You must have him vetted. The veterinary surgeon will give him a complete physical examination and let you know exactly what the current condition of the horse is. Don't expect the animal to be 100 per cent perfect; very, very few are. But as long as the horse's physical problems are small ones and the vet is aware of the sort of work you intend to use him for and gives an okay on that, then it's fine to go ahead.

Remember, it takes an expert eye to see whether a horse is sound or not, and there are some conditions even the vet can't see – only an x-ray examination will reveal them. So be prepared to pay a modest professional fee rather than risk throwing away a much larger sum of money through an avoidable mistake.

Thirdly, don't buy the first horse you see – at least, not until you have inspected a number of others as well. It's not a purchase you want to hurry, and you will be more confident in your final choice if it is the best out of many seen, rather than just two or three.

While we advise you to look at as many horses as you can, there are two areas absolutely to avoid unless the person advising you is *extremely* experienced. These are the horse sale and the horse-dealer. Clearly there are going to be a number of 'good buys' at a sale. Equally, there will be a number of unsound or bad-tempered horses that you may very well fail to recognise, so steer clear of what seems to be the quick, cheap buy.

Horse-dealers should be approached with caution. To go back to our earlier analogy, you can put a marvellous polish and shine on to an old car, but all too soon the engine gives out and you're left with a large pile of scrap metal. Sadly, all too often the same thing can apply to an animal purchased from a horse-dealer, so don't buy from one unless you are recommended by previously satisfied customers. There are, of course, highly reputable dealers, but the prices they ask tend to be on the high side too.

Fourthly, if you have no personal contacts and no previous knowledge of reputable dealers in your area, you will have to consult the advertisements in a responsible journal – *Horse and Hound* will probably be your choice, with literally hundreds of horses and ponies for sale through its columns.

From the brief details given there, you may be able to narrow the choice down to two or three advertisers. Get in touch with them (by telephone, in the first instance) and get more information about the horses you think might suit you. Find out breed, age, height, temperament, training, experience and, of course, price.

If you think you've found a possible buy, you must then arrange to see the horse. Take your expert adviser with you and take your time inspecting the horse. Ask as many questions as you like. You will certainly need answers to the following questions:

1. Is the horse easy to catch?
   Have the horse let out into the paddock or field and see it caught up, then you'll know.

2. Is it traffic proof?
   There is likely to be a road nearby and you can watch the horse being exercised on a road used by traffic. You'll soon see if he is quiet or not.

3. Does the horse take kindly to shoeing and clipping?

4. Does the horse box easily?
Ask to see him led in and out of a travelling box.

5. Has he any stable vices?
Some of the common vices are wind sucking, weaving and crib biting.

A wind sucker grabs with his teeth the top of his stable door or a rail in the field and literally sucks in air and, in so doing, makes gulping noises. It's well nigh impossible to cure this habit successfully. The horse loses condition and, in extreme cases, can refuse to eat and therefore gradually die of starvation. In any event, it is not easy to keep the horse looking at all well.

A weaver displays his symptoms by standing with feet apart and swinging his head from side to side over the stable door. Hardened cases do it behind the door or sometimes in a field. Compulsive weavers will inevitably lose condition after a time but some horses only weave at feed times and when they're excited. In this case, the problem is not too grave. A means of prevention in the stable is to place a v-shaped grid within the upper part of the door. This will prevent the horse from weaving at least within the door area, which is important because horses tend to copy each other and one weaver inside a stable block will possibly affect his companions.

The crib biter will bite and chew up anything wooden in sight. The only immediate answer is to invest in a brick or concrete stable, but liberal coatings of creosote on the wood will help to deter him.

Now all these stable vices are created by boredom. Generally, a highly strung animal starts them; other horses first watch, then follow the habit. Clearly, therefore, it's not a good idea to make your horse purchase from horses afflicted by any of these problems.

Getting answers to all these questions will take time, but however much time and trouble this costs the vendor, do not feel that you are under a moral obligation to recompense him by buying the horse. If you are not 100 per cent certain that the horse is right for you, or if the vet does not wholeheartedly recommend the purchase, firmly say, 'No'. And remember the old saying 'Caveat Emptor' ('Buyer Beware!') – it is up to you to find any faults, not up to the seller to tell you anything you don't ask about.

Now at about this time the word *conformation* may be moving through the conversation, and like any good theme it's open to many variations. By conformation we mean the look and movement of the animal or, in other words, his make and shape. The way that a horse is put together will largely govern the way that he moves, and if a horse moves with a good, free-flowing action and is, as they say in the horse world, 'a good sit-on', that is, he is a nice horse to ride, he will make your efforts to ride him correctly so much easier.

So, what are we looking for in the horse when we first try to weigh him up? Are we really going to like him and get on with him? He has to have a nice temperament, to be, as you might say, a nice person, with a pleasant disposition, easy to get along with and no bad temper about him. So to try to make up our minds about that, we obviously have to look first at his head. Look at his face. Has he got a large, kind eye and an honest expression. A nice width of forehead between his eyes? A nice open, broad nostril? In short, does he have a nice face? Is it a face that you would like? Avoid the very nervy, shifty horse that runs away from every movement. He might be a very straight, honest horse but then again he might have had some very bad treatment in his life and if he's naturally frightened of human beings, you'll be taking a bit of a chance hoping to succeed where others have failed.

Look for a good head carriage and a good, strong neck well set on to a good, strong, sloping shoulder. The head should be well set on to the neck, which should be not too thick through the gullet. If the horse is very thick through his neck and throat, it will be difficult to get him to bridle correctly, to be collected and in a good shape. He would

'A nice face'.

55

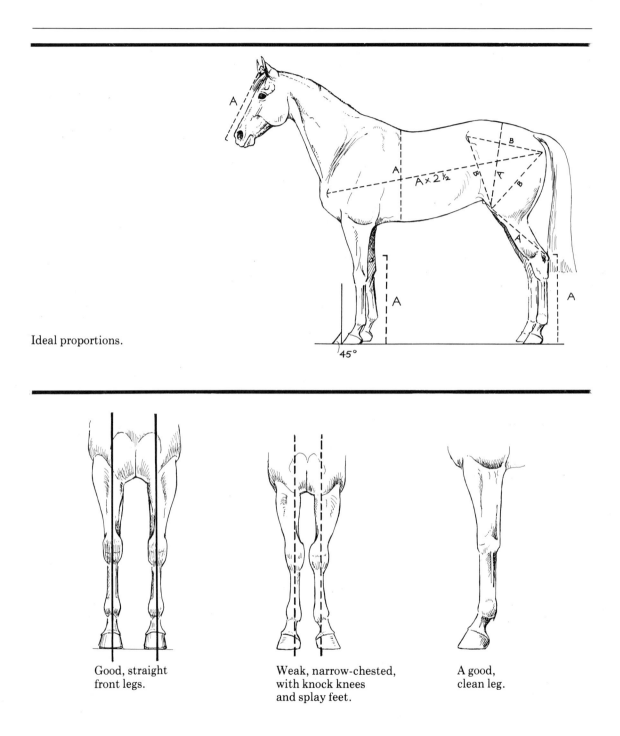

Ideal proportions.

Good, straight
front legs.

Weak, narrow-chested,
with knock knees
and splay feet.

A good,
clean leg.

certainly be difficult to ride with a light, delicate touch on the reins. You should feel that there is always plenty in front of you when you're sitting in the saddle, so we'd like a clearly defined wither and a deep girth, giving plenty of heart room and therefore stamina. There should also be plenty of space to put the saddle, and he should not be a weak, narrow sort of horse, with 'both legs coming out of one hole'. From the front, he wants to be broad across his chest with straight front legs and flat knees, sloping pasterns (about 45 degrees) and well-made feet. The old saying, 'no foot, no horse' is very relevant, for if a horse has bad feet – soft, brittle, flat or boxy – then he's unlikely to stay sound for very long.

A horse with a short back is probably going to be easier for a novice to hold together than a long-backed horse, but in any event he should have strong hind-quarters, a rounded backside and hind legs with large, strong, clean hocks with no lumps or blemishes on them. (Your vet will tell you about all these points.)

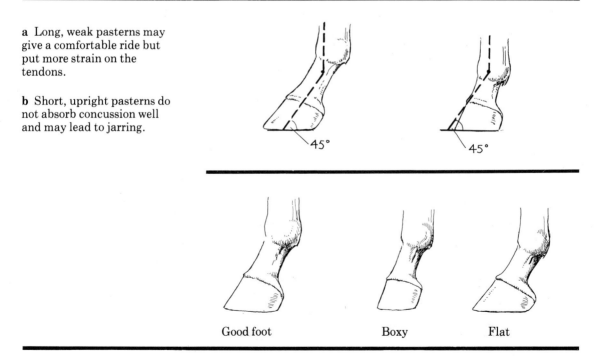

a Long, weak pasterns may give a comfortable ride but put more strain on the tendons.

b Short, upright pasterns do not absorb concussion well and may lead to jarring.

45°   45°

Good foot   Boxy   Flat

Have the horse walked away from you and trotted back towards you, and look to see if he moves straight and freely. Does he turn a foot out or, worse still, both front feet out, or, as we say, 'dish'? If he is a straight mover and looks really good, he is likely to be a better horse to ride. And if he looks smart on the end of a head-collar, and rides well, one day, when you outgrow him, he's going to sell himself to somebody else, isn't he? If he's a bad, scratchy mover, he's unlikely to be a good ride and somebody else, when the day comes when you might want to pass him on, is likely to think the same thing.

When you're thinking of saying 'Yes'

It is astonishingly easy to make a bad decision when you are yearning to say the word that will get you, for the very first time, a horse of your own!

It may seem a silly question, but are you *quite* sure you can afford it? In this respect, a horse is rather like a car. Compared with the running costs you're incurring, the purchase price is trivial. Have you really taken into account all the food, vet's fees, insurance, equipment, shoeing and all the rest of it? If in doubt, play safe – give yourself time to do all the sums again before you commit yourself to 'Yes'!

There's another reason for holding back. Exactly *why* are you thinking of saying 'Yes'? Is it because the horse has such appealing eyes? That may be a reason for picking a kitten, but it's a disastrous way to choose a horse. Is it, on the other hand, because the horse looks so miserable – so much in need of the good home that you're just about to offer the poor old thing? All we have to say about this is: 'Don't be so daft.' The feeling does you credit, but there is very little chance of doing a good turn to a horse in a bad state, and it will be a very bad turn you're doing yourself. Curb those sentimental feelings, and look for the horse that's *right* for you.

Is it the right size? If you are small, you don't want a very large horse. It will be more tiring to groom and more costly to feed. If you're buying for a child, don't buy one a size too large in the hope that the child will 'grow into it' (like a vest). Buy one the right size, and replace it when the child has grown out of it. Don't forget that, when a child has to part with a much-loved pony, this is a somewhat grief-stricken day. Make sure that Pony Number One has a good home to go to, and try to ensure that Pony Number Two arrives, if at all possible, before the other one leaves.

Now ask yourself if the horse you're thinking of buying is the right age. You may be tempted by a young and mettlesome steed, but it will almost certainly be more than the first-time owner can possibly cope with. A good rule is to avoid buying any horse less than eight years old; better still, go for one that is nine, ten or eleven. After all, in the partnership between you and your horse, it is only right that his experience should make up for your own inexperience. A horse too young to have learned much will not be able to teach you much, and you could both end up being very confused and unhappy. Don't be persuaded to buy a younger horse (that's one between three and six years) even though you may be told that he's very quiet and easy. The chances are that he has not yet reached maturity and is therefore likely to start experimenting to see how far he can go with you – which could cause long-term complications for both of you.

One last, rather indefinite point: how can you make sure that you make no mistake when you're buying your first horse? If you just want a horse for gentle hacking around country lanes, you'll want one with a suitable set of characteristics. If you have show-jumping ambitions, you'll want a quite different kind of horse. If you'll be riding him much on roads, you want a horse that will behave well in traffic. It is even possible that you will choose a horse that seems – and indeed is – exactly right for you in every way, and then find that you and he have utterly incompatible temperaments. That could be a disastrous mistake – how could you put it right?

Fortunately, there *is* a way. If you are buying from someone who really wants you to get all the pleasure and satisfaction you're looking for and, at the same time, be certain that the horse is going to a good home, you should be able to reach a kind of 'on approval' agreement. That is to say, for two or three weeks after buying the horse you will have the chance of finding out whether you've made a mistake, and, if you have, returning the horse and getting your money back. This is perfectly reasonable, but the selling owner would quite naturally insist upon a proper insurance policy to cover the horse against any fatality or disablement. Also, it would be in both your interests to have a written agreement covering the situation. You will, of course, also have to play the game. If, during the two or three weeks in your care, the horse falls ill or has an accident, you cannot then say that you don't want him and would like your money back.

But now let us suppose that you have avoided all the pitfalls lying in wait for you. You've bought the horse, and we just hope the choice is right. As you have not previously been a horse-owner, you presumably don't have a horse-box. So you arrange for him to be delivered. It's quite likely that the vendor will organise transport for you, using his own box. But if that is impossible you should make your own arrangements with a livestock transport firm. These carriers tend to be expensive – they have a living to make – but expense is the name of the game. Horses are just that!

It is vital, before you take charge of your new purchase, that you have him insured. There's a scheme run through the British Horse Society which is perfectly sound and which we recommend, and of course normal insurance brokers will offer quotations to you. Of course, you'll get the sort of insurance cover you pay for. Should your horse have a fatal accident, no amount of money your insurance company pays out will replace that friend you've lost, but at least you'll be able to buy another horse and build up a new friendship.

Where should you keep your horse?

There are three possibilities, and you will obviously have made arrangements well in advance.

At livery

You can keep your horse 'at livery'. A livery stable is, so to speak, a horse's hotel. This method gives you the very minimum of work and trouble, but the result is that it costs you more. You have to pay for your horse's food and equipment, of course, and also your share of the cost of a paid staff and the livery stable's overheads. If this is the only way in which you can keep a horse of your own (and you can afford it), there's nothing to be said against it; but you're sure to find that visiting a horse (even every day) is not quite the same thing as having your horse to live with you.

There is, in financial terms, an advantageous variation to the full-livery system, and this is known as *part-livery*. The horse enjoys all the conditions of being kept at livery but is available to the stable owner for his use, whether in terms of hiring out for hacking or, with your agreement, for hunting, or even in the local show rings. So part-livery, in actual fact, means that you only part-own your horse in a practical sense, and others will be riding him. So you weigh up the financial considerations of having the horse for your exclusive use as against sharing him.

At grass

You can keep your horse 'at grass', that is to say, your horse lives in a field. This is not necessarily a disadvantage. A horse is not a domestic pet, and its ancestors lived very successfully in the wild. It's also reasonably economical . . . but, in the winter months, limiting. Hard riding is totally out of the question, for the horse turned out into a cold winter field in a hot and sweaty condition is almost certainly going to catch a chill, with all the problems that can result in. Be prepared during the winter months to reduce your riding to daily slow hacking but, in any event, you must not turn your horse into just any old field.

You will need an area of about two acres, and the field must be safe. That is to say, it must be securely fenced, with a gate that fastens securely. The very best fencing is post and rail, using good, seasoned, strong wood. There's no doubt that the ideally fenced field would have three sides made of post and rail and the fourth side of a good, strong, secure, well-tended hedge. The hedge, of course,

Good post and rail fencing with a self-filling water trough. (If this fence were not dividing two fields but simply around one, the rails would be nailed onto the insides of the posts to prevent them being pushed off by a horse rubbing or leaning against them.)

provides the necessary shelter and if there is no natural shelter in the field, you will have to provide a roomy shed, open on one side (preferably the south), to shelter the horse from rain, wind and sun. Barbed wire, or indeed plain wire, is not satisfactory and should be avoided if at all possible. If, on the other hand, you have no choice but to use wire, make sure that the strands are well off the ground and are always in a taut condition. This type of fencing requires constant inspection because it offers dangers that post and rail or good hedging avoids. The field must also possess a continuous supply of water. At the very best, this source would be provided by a fresh water stream or a self-filling water trough. But whatever system you have to use, it is of absolute importance that the supply of water is constant and adequate, and do remember that in the winter water freezes over and horses are unable to break thick ice. You will have to do that job every day there is a heavy frost.

Remember that the grass in your horse's field is not just for walking on and rolling on. It's also his food supply for most of the year. You will have to see that there is plenty of good quality grass in fine condition throughout the growing season. And this of course means hard work, with yearly 'topping' of weeds to make sure the pasture remains more grass than nettle or dock, and picking up the droppings on a regular basis, because these sour the grass and the horse won't touch those areas. He's a very choosy feeder and you'll quickly notice that large areas of pasture are not to his liking. It is very beneficial, therefore, to ring changes and try to arrange with neighbours for their cattle to graze the pasture while your horse is feeding elsewhere. The field quickly becomes 'horse-sick' if your animal lives on it year round. Necessary also to the condition of the paddock is regular periods of resting when the pasture is allowed to grow and restore itself.

If you have no alternative, there is a system known as strip grazing. You simply divide whatever area of paddock or pasture you have into two by means of an electric fence. If you adopt this method, make sure you introduce your horse to the fence by walking him around the new boundaries.

One last thing to keep in mind when you're looking for a paddock big enough for your horse is that a horse on his own gets lonely. So it would be sensible to allow room for at least one more horse – that's three to four acres in all.

Stabled at home

The third method of keeping horses is in every way the best, if you have the resources. This is to have your own horse in your stables conveniently close to your own house. This doesn't mean that you have to live in a castle or a stately home; farms, country rectories, houses built for quite modestly landed gentry a hundred years ago all had to have accommodation for horses when mechanical transport was rare or non-existent. A great many families have the space, and often the buildings, to keep horses comfortably and efficiently if they really want to.

Will you really want to?

63

This may seem an odd question to ask, but you can't answer it without visualising exactly what you're taking on. Will you want to groom your horse every day – yes, *every* day – once the novelty has worn off? Will you rise to the occasion when you have to nurse a sick horse or give first-aid to an injured one? Does the idea of mucking out a stable every day put you off? Will you give your horse a bucket of clean water three or four times a day? That means you'll be humping about two tons of water in the course of a year as well as shifting more than two tons of hay – will it be too much for you? Will you really want to do all that work?

This picture gives you an idea of the amount of gear you will need for your horse. Not all these items are on your list of essentials, but you will probably accumulate them sooner or later!

We're writing this book for people who will answer: 'Of *course* I want to!' Those are the people who will find that caring for horses gives just as much satisfaction as riding them – more, perhaps.

This list contains the essential gear you must buy before your horse arrives.

Head-collar
Lead rope
Grooming kit – dandy brush, body brush, water brush, rubber or plastic curry comb, curry comb, mane and tail comb, stable rubber, hoof pick, small plastic bucket and two sponges.
First aid kit
Saddle and numnah, girth, leathers, stirrups, treads
Bridle and bit
Jute rug (or equivalent for use in stable)
New Zealand rug for use in field
Blanket for use under rug in very cold weather
Sweat rug
Tack-cleaning equipment – saddle soap, oil, sponge, cloth
Feed bucket (if no manger or old ceramic sink available)
Water bucket (preferably metal)
Hay nets (2)
*Saddle and bridle rack
*Saddle-cleaning stand and bridle hook
    *Both preferable but not absolutely essential
Fork, shovel, broom, barrow, skip
Hoof oil and brush
Feed storage bins – galvanised
Feed scoop
Feed, hay and straw

Stable routines

Even if you have to face the fact that having a horse of your own in a stable of your own may still be a long way off, there is a lot to be gained by taking the trouble to *understand* the care of horses, even if you meet them only two or three times a week, and it will do no harm at all to imagine what it will be like when your own horse is living in your own stable . . .

Your horse will have a roomy box, preferably about four metres square, light and airy and free from draughts. The door opens in two halves, so that the bottom half can be shut to keep the horse in, while the top half stays open so that the horse can get plenty of fresh air and can look out, see what is going on in the stable yard and have some notice taken of him – by you. Horses are both inquisitive and sociable, so it's very important to let them feel that they are part of the community. Talking to horses, patting their necks and stroking their muzzles are not signs of sentimentality; they are essential means of communicating your feelings to the horse – signalling friendship, in fact.

There are some other features of this stable of yours. The horse's bedding is the most noticeable. There are several different materials that can be used, but many people would recommend wheat straw as the best. It is also of course the most readily available and is reasonably cheap, but perhaps its most important benefit is that it is easily disposable. Straw muck makes excellent garden fertilizer and if you find yourself living near to a mushroom farm then the owners will be delighted to make your acquaintance. There are, however, some very acceptable alternatives. Wood shavings are used by many people, although they are difficult to dispose of. Peat is very expensive, but easily obtainable. It's good for the garden anyway, and will obviously be even better when the horse has finished with it. Shredded paper has also become popular recently, and it's a good choice for a horse that eats straw and thus eats its bed unless you use another material. So by making use of either shavings, peat or shredded paper you immediately have more control over your horse's diet. A greedy horse will have eaten a large quantity of his bedding by morning; his waistline will suffer and so will his wind. It is essential to steer clear of straw if your horse suffers from respiratory or 'wind' problems, for through eating straw he will inhale the dust which in turn will aggravate his throat and produce a dry cough and problems to which there is no other answer than to replace his bedding.

The muck heap

In the summer months, flies are a constant irritation to horses, so don't aggravate the problem by placing your muck heap next door to the stable. But if you put it too far away, then you will wear yourself out wheeling that barrow back and forth. When you've decided upon a location for it, make sure that it's in a well-sheltered area, because a good wind can move the entire muck heap overnight. As with everything else concerning stable management, keep the muck heap nicely squared and tidied.

Water and hay

Make sure your horse has a constant supply of water in his stable at all times with but one exception: do not make a full bucket available to him when he comes into his stable extremely hot and sweaty after exercise. His natural inclination will be to drink the entire bucket of cold water and this will very likely upset his stomach and produce the onset of colic. But if he has gone a long time without water (for example, after a day's hunting), offer him a *small* drink of water with some hot added to take the chill off. You can then give him a bran mash (see p.115) or some hay and another small drink an hour or so later.

Make sure that hay is always available to him as long as he's not too overweight. A horse naturally eats all the time and this munching relieves his boredom and has the bonus of saving on too much hard food. The hard food diet, remember, makes him very fresh and larky. There are a number of ways of presenting the hay to your horse: one is by use of a hay net. If you use this method, make sure the net is hung at a sufficient height to prevent the horse's feet becoming entangled in it when it's empty. Alternatively, you can feed hay in a rack at head height or in a rack at chest height, which comes in the form of a low manger into which the hay is dropped. We believeit to be a far better idea for the horse to eat with his head lowered. Not only is it his natural eating position, but since all your riding hours are spent encouraging the horse to keep his head bent or lowered, we think it is rather foolish to contradict this constant request by letting him eat with his head high in the air. We don't object to the idea of his eating off the stable floor as long as the floor is clean and he eats up all he's given, but if hay is wasted on the stable floor, then you are wasting money.

Daily routines

General routine in the morning

1 General check on the well-being of your horse (perhaps he's knocked himself during the night).
2 Check and adjust the rugs (if they're being used).
3 Muck out.
4 Quarter the horse.
5 Water, feed and replenish hay.

Now let's have a look at the daily chores starting with the morning mucking out. Remember that horses like to have familiar routines (like many children). They feel more settled if the same thing happens at the same time every day. So, if your horse is used to seeing you at 6.30 a.m., don't let him down by having a lie-in until 7.30 just because you feel lazy on an icy winter morning!

Walk into your horse's stable and check that he is all right. You'll notice that the bedding is wet (when people do it, it's urinating, when horses do it, it's 'staling'). There will also be droppings. The first task is to separate clean and soiled bedding with your pitchfork, the clean being piled up against the stable wall and the dirty taken to the muck heap.

As often as possible, allow the box to air and the floor to dry out. If conditions permit, have the horse tied up outside the box while this takes place. Whatever happens, do not leave your horse standing on a bare, damp floor. It is definitely bad for his legs and recent research suggests it's also bad for his respiration. Fumes of ammonia rising from the floor could be the cause of this. Do make sure that all damp straw is removed from the stables. If you leave it in, diseases can occur in the feet, the most troublesome of which is called thrush and is a fungal infection. (If your horse should get thrush – which he can also get from standing in a wet and muddy field if you don't pick his feet out every day – clean his feet three times a day, brushing-out and then applying Stockholm tar well into the frog area and cleft of the heels – or spray well with purple antiseptic spray into all cracks and crevices.)

Next you pick out the horse's feet. This means using a hoof pick to clean out dirty bedding from round the frog. This is followed by 'quartering', which is a quick tidy-up in contrast to the main grooming (known as strapping). It involves brushing the horse all over lightly; sponging eyes, nostrils and dock; damping down the mane and tail; oiling the hooves with hoof oil. Now put the horse's bed down and give him a bucket of fresh water, followed by the first feed of the day. *Remember that at least an hour must elapse between the end of the feed and starting any exercise.*

Quartering the horse

1 Rack (i.e. tie him up).
2 Remove the rug (partially if cold).
3 Pick out his feet.
4 Brush all over with a body brush (use a dandy brush if your horse has not been clipped).
5 Sponge the eyes, the nose and the dock.
6 Damp the mane and tail.
7 Apply hoof oil both on the outer and inner part of the horse's hooves (this is not absolutely necessary during the afternoon grooming).
8 Re-rug him or, if you're about to ride, tack him up.

We have suggested that you quarter your horse first thing in the morning, but you could do it after he has been fed and before your morning ride. The main grooming is done after exercise (either immediately on return or some time during the afternoon) and takes the best part of an hour, all of it hard work. Here is a summary of what you have to do.

First, you tie the horse up to a ring or post with a length of *string*. If, for some reason, he is startled and shies, the string will break. In this way, you avoid any risk of the horse injuring himself. Then you pick out his feet again to get rid of mud and stones. Check his shoes – one may have worked loose during exercise, or clenches may have risen. That means you call in the farrier.

If it's a wet day, the horse's legs will be muddy, so dry them off with a towel or handful of straw, paying particular attention to the heels. Damp heels can turn into cracked heels. You can either wash the horse (but only in warm weather), making sure that he is completely dry before you brush him, or you can let the mud dry on him, and get it off with the stiff-bristled dandy brush. On a dry day, go straight to work with the dandy brush, and remove the dirt and sweat-marks from his legs and the less sensitive parts of his body. You may wonder how you know the less sensitive parts, especially as these can vary from horse to horse (just as some people are more ticklish than others). Don't worry. If the dandy brush makes the horse uncomfortable at any stage in the proceeding, he will let you know.

The softer body brush is now used to give the horse a complete brushing from head to tail. You will have the curry comb in the other hand and use it to clean hairs and dust from the body brush every few strokes. Never use the dandy brush or curry comb on mane or tail – only the body brush. This is because the hair of the mane and tail breaks easily, and a stiff brush would damage it.

Next comes the stable rubber folded into a soft pad to give the horse an invigorating massage. Use a gentle 'thumping' action on his neck and quarters, toning up his muscles and stimulating his circulation.

Next sponge eyes, nostrils and mouth. Then, using a second sponge kept for this alone, sponge the dock.

Pick out the feet, moving the hoof pick only in the direction shown (from heel to toe) in order to avoid the chance of damaging the sensitive frog; oil both underneath and on the outside of the hoof.

Next the water brush: it looks much like the dandy brush but has softer bristles and is used to lay the mane. Damp (not wet), it brushes the hair of the mane to one side of the horse's neck.

Next, the stable rubber is used again to go over the entire horse and give him a final 'polish'.

Finally, brush the hooves with hoof oil again, inside and out.

Now the horse gets another bucket of fresh water and his second (or third) feed of the day.

A quick guide to the day's routine

7.00 a.m. Water, check rugs and welfare of the horse.
7.15 Muck out and sweep up.
7.30 Feed and hay (if you're putting hay on the floor, wait until you've mucked out).
8.00 Breakfast for the owner. (Not to be taken until the horse has been fed.)
8.30 Quarter the horse.
8.45 Ride.
10.00 Make the horse comfortable in the stable.
12.30 Lunchtime hard feed and/or hay. Skip out (remove the droppings).
3.00 Groom (on a pleasant day, turn the horse out for an hour and a half before you groom him).
4.30 Skip out and tidy the yard.
5.00 Evening feed and hay. If it's possible, check on your horse's need for extra hay and water before you go to bed.

Washing your horse

You can only wash your horse on a very mild day in spring or summer. If the horse is sweating, then, rather like you, he'd appreciate a shower. So, either hose him down or wash him with a bucket and sponge. If you choose to use a bucket of water, then take the chill off it. Do pay particular attention to the folds of skin between his front legs and around the sheath area. Wash between the back legs but avoid wetting his loins unless it's a really hot day, and even on these days, after washing down, scrape the excess water off with a sweat scraper and then walk him gently about wearing a sweat rug to help him dry off. In the winter, he must not, under any circumstances, be washed. Chills – colds – are a great risk. The most you can do is to sponge his face, between his legs and on the saddle patch. Then, rub all those areas vigorously with an old towel or with dry, clean straw. Then 'thatch him up'. It's a very apt way of describing what you do. Take a generous armful of straw, lay it over his back, put the rug on top of the straw (inside out so that if it gets damp you are not putting the inside on his body when you take the straw out) and then fasten in the usual way. This allows the air to pass through the straw beneath the rug and gently and gradually dry him out without any chance of his catching a chill. Alternatively (especially if the horse is kept on shavings and there is no straw available), put the sweat rug on with the jute rug inside out over it. Leave the front undone, folded up and fastened under a roller. This will allow air to circulate round the chest area, keep the loins warm and let the horse's skin 'breathe' through the jute.

Tack

This is a suitable place to consider the 'tack' or 'saddlery' – the equipment that is fitted on the horse when you ride him – because that, too, is involved in the daily cleaning routine.

The main parts of the equipment are the saddle and bridle, and we'll give you a simple description of these and explain their functions. We say 'simple' because there are many different types of saddle and a great variety of bridles, some extremely elaborate and complicated. There is, of course, a real purpose in every variation, but explaining them all will not help you to the basic understanding that is our main purpose.

A good quality saddle and bridle with a snaffle bit. The stirrups are correctly run up the leathers so that they will not slide down.

The saddle is the seat for the rider. The bridle is fitted to the horse's head and incorporates the bit. The bit is put into the horse's mouth and connected to the rider's hands by the reins.

This therefore constitutes the mechanism by which the rider controls the horse, as described in the first part of this book.

One of the functions of the saddle is to protect the rider from the discomfort of bouncing up and down on the horse's spine, and the other is to protect the horse from the discomfort of having his spine bounced on by several kilos

73

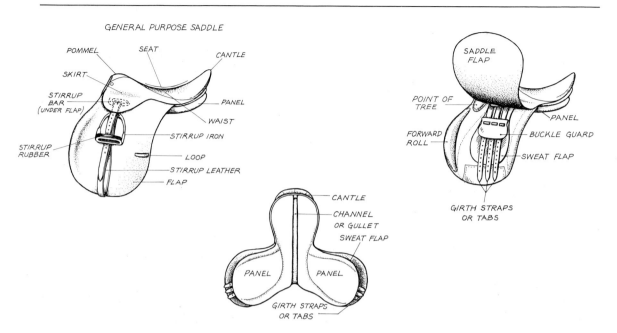

GENERAL PURPOSE SADDLE

POMMEL
SEAT
CANTLE
SKIRT
STIRRUP BAR (UNDER FLAP)
PANEL
WAIST
STIRRUP IRON
STIRRUP RUBBER
LOOP
STIRRUP LEATHER
FLAP

SADDLE FLAP
POINT OF TREE
PANEL
FORWARD ROLL
BUCKLE GUARD
SWEAT FLAP
GIRTH STRAPS OR TABS

CANTLE
CHANNEL OR GULLET
SWEAT FLAP
PANEL
PANEL
GIRTH STRAPS OR TABS

SNAFFLE BRIDLE

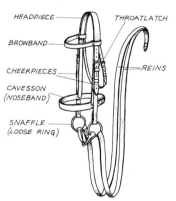

HEADPIECE
THROATLATCH
BROWBAND
CHEEKPIECES
REINS
CAVESSON (NOSEBAND)
SNAFFLE (LOOSE RING)

of human. The saddle is constructed on a framework known as the 'saddle tree', which fits onto the horse's rib cage and does not bear on the spine at all, provided it is well designed and a good fit for the horse on which it is used. If it is well designed, it makes it quite hard for the rider to sit anywhere but dead centre, where he should be. You should know that the back of the saddle, which slopes upward to support the base of your spine, is called the 'cantle', and the front, or 'pommel', is the bit you clutch at in the early stages of learning to ride when you think you're just going to fall off!

On each side of the saddle are stirrup leathers, straps supporting the stirrup irons in which you put your feet. The stirrup leathers are adjustable, and it's obviously important that, when you mount your horse, you ensure that the leathers are correctly adjusted for your length of leg (see p.29).

The girth is the strap that is buckled to each side of the saddle, going underneath the horse and holding the saddle in place. It is very important indeed to adjust the girth (see p.29) before you move off. If the girth is too tight, it's uncomfortable for the horse; if it's too loose, the saddle slips to one side and the rider falls off.

A bridle with a cavesson noseband, onto which is attached a standing martingale. *Never* attach a standing martingale to a drop noseband, as this would exert too much pressure and affect the horse's breathing.

A bridle showing a drop noseband and running martingale. The rubber or leather stops prevent the rings on the martingale from sliding up the reins and hitting the bit.

Now for the bridle. This is an arrangement of straps around the horse's head. There is a headpiece, which goes over the head behind the ears. The browband is attached to the headpiece and goes across the forehead. The cheekpieces are also attached to the headpiece, lying along the horse's cheeks and performing the very important function of holding the bit. The throatlash is part of the headpiece and crosses the horse's throat. Its function is to keep the bridle on.

The reins are attached to the bit. And there is sometimes, but not invariably, a noseband, some types of which – those which are done up below the bit – help to keep the horse's mouth closed. Higher up on the jaw bone, a cavesson noseband acts in much the same way with the added advantage that a standing martingale may be attached to it. This and the running martingale help to control the horse's head position and movements.

Now, before we describe the process of fitting the equipment onto the horse ('tacking up'), we should answer a question that just might be in your mind. When you buy your horse, does he come with all this gear? Or is he naked until you go shopping on his behalf? It could be either. The animal you buy could well be sold with all his tack complete, especially if he is an outgrown pony, whose tack will not fit his replacement. If the tack is of good quality and neither damaged nor too worn, this is an ideal solution. You can generally assume that the tack fits the horse and that he feels comfortable with it.

But people usually want to retain the tack, so if they seem at all anxious to sell it with the horse, do make sure that the saddle really does fit and doesn't need re-stuffing. Make sure the rest of the tack is in good, supple condition. If you are in any doubt, then take all the tack to a saddler for him to check out and guarantee as sound.

If you have to buy the tack yourself, you will be well advised to observe once more the two Golden Rules: deal only with the most reputable firms (the best saddlers are extremely well known in the world of the horse) and buy the very best quality that you can afford. Buying poor tack is an 'economy' that you will be sure to regret. At best it will wear out quickly and at worst it will be a positive danger.

Tacking up   Imagine now that you have solved all these preliminary
problems, and that you are about to tack up your own
horse for the very first time.

Tie him up to a post or ring or to the stable door, using a
head-collar *and* the loop of string that, in the case of
accidents, will break before any damage is done. *Put the
bridle on first.* Obviously by doing this the horse is
immediately more manageable and should he get loose
while tacking up, then clearly, with the bridle on, it's much
easier to catch him again.

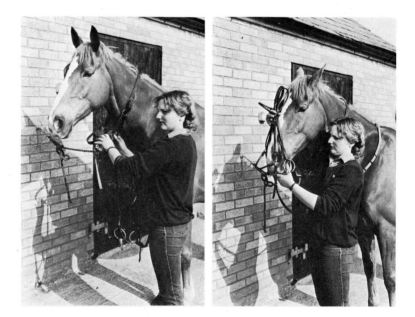

Stand on the horse's near side. Remove the head-collar
and buckle it round his neck. Put the reins over his head so
that they hang on his neck. Hold the headpiece in the right
hand and the bit in the left hand. You are going to draw the
bridle up onto the horse's head (rather like pulling on a
sock, with the bit representing the toe), the first step being
the insertion of the bit in his mouth. Face forwards and put
your right arm under the horse's jaw to hold the bridle,
while the left hand gently persuades the horse to open his
mouth by putting the thumb into the corner of the mouth
where there are no teeth. Now insert the bit.

The bit is positioned over the tongue and lies on the 'bars' of the horse's mouth; those are the parts of his lower jaw between his front teeth and his back teeth. Be careful not to knock the bit against his teeth or make it in any way an uncomfortable or disagreeable experience. In very cold weather, it's a kind action to warm the bit before putting it in the horse's mouth. Always remember that it is the sensitivity of the horse's mouth that is the essential link in the passing of those subtle signals from mind to hands to mouth to mind.

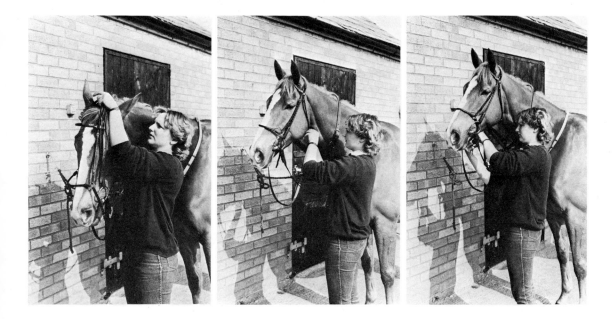

With the bit in position, you pull the headpiece up and over the horse's ears, pulling the forelock over the browband and checking that every part is now correctly positioned.

Start tightening all the buckles, beginning with noseband and throatlash – neither of them being too tight. There should be room for a fist between throat and throatlash, and room for two fingers between nose and noseband. Check finally that the bridle is straight by looking at it from the front. Check that the bit is high enough in the mouth to create a couple of wrinkles on either side. Make sure that the horse is comfortable and that the loose ends of all straps are in their keepers and runners. Now put the head-collar back on the horse's head over the bridle.

Now you're ready to put on the saddle. Numnahs are best used under saddles to protect and cushion the horse's back, and to protect the underside of the saddle from the horse's sweat. Put the saddle high on the horse's withers and slide it back into position so that the hairs on his back are not rubbed up the wrong way.

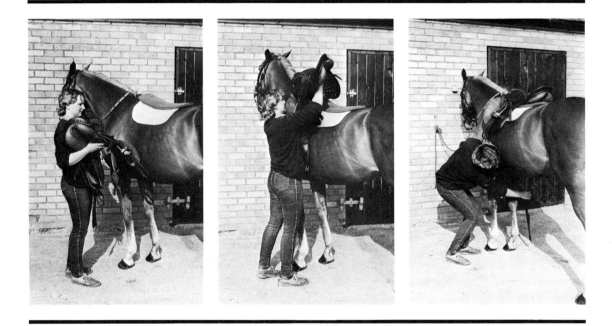

Note the reins hooked under
the run-up stirrups to stop
them coming over the horse's
head and getting tangled with
its feet should it put its head
down.

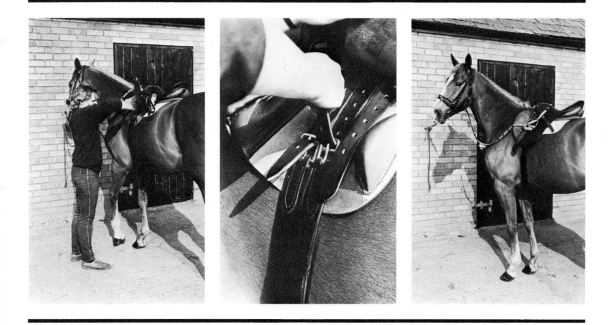

Check both sides of the saddle before fastening the girth
to make sure that flaps and straps have not become tucked
up. Remember that the girth will be finally adjusted when
you mount. The stirrup irons will remain hitched up at the
tops of the leathers ('run up') until you're ready to mount.
Otherwise they could bang your shins while you're carrying
the saddle, or annoy the horse as you put the saddle on.
They will be 'run down' as you prepare to mount, and
finally adjusted when you're in the saddle.

79

Untacking

This is obviously quicker and easier than tacking up, but it still has to be done correctly. Put the head-collar on the horse over the bridle and tie him up. Always take the saddle off first because this is the most burdensome piece of tack the horse has to carry (which is why we have stressed good fit and comfort as far as the saddle is concerned). Furthermore, the horse's back could well want airing if the saddle patch is hot and sweaty. And, of course, if he runs off, the expensive saddle is in great danger.

The girth should have been loosened already and the stirrup irons run up. Then unbuckle the girth on the near side. When it hangs loose, move round to the off side and lay the girth across the saddle. Come back to the near side and lift the saddle off, still moving it in the direction of the hair. Don't just sling your saddle down onto the ground. It's a very valuable piece of tack, so either put it over a door, or stand it well away from the horse to save him having a nibble at it, putting it gently down on its front end with the numnah or the girth protecting the pommel from scratching on stones or concrete.

Before you take the bridle off, remove the head-collar and attach it round the horse's neck, so that you still have control as you remove the bridle. Hang the reins on the horse's neck. Undo the buckles of throatlash and noseband. Lift the headpiece and reins over the ears so that you can slide the bridle off altogether. Take the bit in the left hand, but let the horse open his mouth and slip the bit out of his own accord. You do not have to pull it out. However, do rinse it immediately you take it from the horse's mouth. It saves quite a bit of cleaning later on. Now put the head-collar back on the horse's head.

That's all that's involved in taking off saddle and bridle, but there's still the checking and cleaning to be done.

Always put your saddle down carefully on its front end or on the pommel with something underneath to protect the leather.

Tack-cleaning and conditioning

Regardless of whether you've bought new or second-hand, all that leather and metal will have been expensive, but it certainly won't look after itself. Each time you use it, you must clean it. Sweat from the horse and, of course, rain, play havoc with the condition of leather and in a relatively short space of time your tack will start to crack and, of course, become dangerous. The cleaning process itself is simple enough but it does take time and a certain amount of energy. But there are no short cuts and it must be done. Saddle soap, which comes in bars or tins, provides on a day-to-day basis all the goodness the leather part of your tack needs. Use ordinary metal polish on the stirrups and buckles to guard against corrosion.

Tack-cleaning is a simple enough process for which you'll need saddle soap, two sponges, one soft cloth, one bucket of lukewarm water, one bowl of lukewarm water, ordinary household soap or washing-up liquid. Wash all the leather parts of the tack with ordinary soap to remove the mud and grime but don't get the leather too wet. Then, dip the saddle soap into the lukewarm water in the clean bowl and wipe the soap onto the sponge. Then cover all the leather with a fine coating of saddle soap and leave it to dry. If you've been caught in the rain, then there's one further process that must be followed. Clean the tack in the way we've described, then use an application of hydrophane or neatsfoot oil to feed condition back into the leather. But don't use these oils on the top of your saddle; underneath only. If you cover the area you sit on, then you're going to leave a stain on your breeches which no amount of washing or dry-cleaning will remove. Both the recommended oils have a further use in helping to soften up new tack or to recondition old tack.

Grooming kit

The items listed below are essential to the external
condition of your horse. They won't cost a fortune, but do
shop around because prices can vary considerably. The list
we've made up is in the exact order you'll use all this
equipment.

1. Dandy brush — This brush is used to remove the mud and loose hairs from the entire coat of the horse.

2. Body brush — Follows the use of the dandy brush and its purpose is to clean and tone the coat.

3. Metal curry comb — Used with the body brush to keep the body brush clean. *Not* used on the horse.

4. Plastic or rubber curry comb — Occasionally used to remove stubborn mud when the dandy brush won't and also used to clean the dandy brush.

5. Water brush — For damping down the mane and tail.

6. Stable rubber — For an extra-fine polish and toning of the coat.

7. Mane and tail comb — Used in the pulling and plaiting of both mane and tail.

8. Hoof pick — This metal object does exactly what its name suggests – the essential process of keeping the underneath part of the hoof clean. It's a very vulnerable area and subject to fungal infections.

9. Ladies' hairbrush — To be used only when your horse has a delicate tail.

10. Two sponges
One sponge to be used for cleaning the eyes and nose and the other to be used for cleaning the dock. Never mix the two up.

11. A small bucket
To hold the water for the sponges. We hope the order of sponge use is obvious, but just in case, eyes and nose first and then, with the second sponge, the dock.

12. Hoof oil
This oil is applied to the horse's hooves to keep them in good condition. It should be used underneath as well as on the top of the hoof.

The grooming kit: (clockwise from bottom left) stable rubber, mane and tail comb, hoof pick, sweat scraper, hoof oil and brush, tail bandage, dandy brush, water brush, sponges, rubber curry comb, body brush, curry comb.

In addition to these essentials, it would be well to have a tin of vaseline standing by to use with an old rag under the tail to prevent dryness and then a bottle of baby oil to use with a clean rag around the eyes and nostrils for a little bit of extra shine. Perhaps a trifle cosmetic, but it does improve the appearance of your horse. Add a pair of sharp scissors to your list. You'll find them very useful for trimming the heels and long hairs on the head and for cutting a two-inch gap from the mane just where the headpiece of the bridle goes over the poll so that the bridle and head-collar will fit more comfortably. However, if your horse is out at grass in wet weather, do not cut the hair in his heels, as he needs the protection. All this trimming can be done with clippers but they are expensive and, unless you know exactly how to use them, the job is best left to professionals. Most riding schools are willing to help out in this area if they have time.

You perhaps noticed one rather odd item on the list above – the ladies' hairbrush. Some horses do have delicate tails which can easily be ruined by using the normal mane and tail comb. The hairs can be pulled out, split or broken, leaving a very ragged item tacked onto the back of your horse. The hairbrush is obviously a much more sympathetic way of helping the tail to retain its shape and appearance.

Now having collected together all this equipment, don't leave it scattered all over the place, but keep it in a bucket or box. The hoof pick, by the way, has an uncanny knack of getting lost. We tie a piece of coloured string to ours to make sure it can't escape so easily. Another tip which we find helps in the grooming process is to put the tail bandage on while you're working over the rest of the horse. We find it helps to lay the tail but don't, for heaven's sake, attempt any mane or tail pulling until you have been thoroughly instructed in how to do it. In fact, with the entire process of grooming your horse, we advise you to visit your local stables regularly and watch how the experts do it. You'll see how all the equipment is used and you'll learn how to use it properly.

The stable

Drum into your head just two words as far as stables are concerned: SAFETY and COMFORT. If you're unable to provide these two basic necessities, then you shouldn't be owning a horse. However, that said, you don't have to provide an equine palace. The stable area must be large enough for the horse to move around easily, lie down and, most importantly of course, get up. The interior walls must be smooth and even – any rough projections could damage the horse. Equally, the floor must be level and solid. The door should be wide enough and high enough for the horse to be led squarely through and made of good solid material. A properly sized door allows you to lead your horse in and out of the stable quietly and safely. If the door is too narrow, or is positioned in such a way that the horse has to turn as soon as he comes out, it's quite likely that the horse will bump himself going through, take fright and tend to try to rush in and out.

That old expression 'locking the stable door' has more than a ring of truth about it. Do make absolutely certain that the fittings that secure the door do just that and make sure that bolts are fitted at the top and bottom of the door. Your horse is an ingenious character and will quickly sort out the way to open his door if the fittings allow him to. With the normal split stable door, the horse, particularly when he's bored, will also be inclined to nibble at the top of the woodwork. We fit a metal plate over the top of the door, making sure, of course, that there are no sharp edges, and we find that this more than adequately frustrates the nibbling habit.

The stable must be well-ventilated but not draughty and the roof must be absolutely waterproof. If the stable opens straight out rather than being in a barn, you should also make sure that there is sufficient roof overhang above the door to prevent the horse's head getting wet when it rains. Perhaps the ideal stable, or loosebox, is the one Steve is standing by in the picture overleaf. This incorporates the most modern ideas in terms of feeding and watering, safety and comfort.

Having satisfied yourself that the horse is safe and

Steve's stables, built by
Loddon Livestock,
incorporate all the most
modern design features. Note
the feed basin, which revolves
so that it can be filled without
entering the stable.

comfortable, the next essentials obviously are food and
drink. Water must be constantly available. Buckets do the
job perfectly well but be careful how you place them. They
don't want to be in the horse's way, so choose a corner of
the stable and carefully wedge the bucket and make it
secure. If you're leaving your horse in the stable for a
longish period of time, say from six in the evening to seven
or eight the following morning, leave two buckets securely
placed in his stable. If he finishes them both off, then you'll
know he's had sufficient water. If he's knocked them over,
then it's tough on him and he'll just have to learn not to. As
far as food goes, a manger is the ideal for feeding hay,
although a properly hung hay net also does the job well.
For the hard foods – oats, bran, nuts, etc. – of course these
can be provided in a bucket or we've often seen, and quite
approve of, an old, deep kitchen sink that has been set up
securely in the stable. In between feeds, your horse can get
bored and a salt lick helps him to while away the time and
of course provides a useful dietary supplement.

Whatever bedding you use, and these days choice ranges
from straw through peat to shredded paper, it must be kept
clean and dry, which means regular mucking out and the
daily removal of droppings. And that can also cause a
problem if you've nowhere to put the muck. If your space is
that limited, make sure that your neighbours will be happy

The inside of the stable, with a good, deep straw bed, hay in a manger in the corner and an automatic waterer on the far wall.

to receive your surplus muck for their roses or kitchen garden. Mucking out is not a job you can do by hand, so make sure that you have available a good-sized wheelbarrow, fork, shovel and a good, hard yard broom. A small skip is quite useful for taking out the odd droppings during the day. No shortcuts please: your horse wants to live in clean, dry, comfortable quarters just as you do – and it's just as essential to his health.

The tack room

In an ideal world, the tack room would be sited alongside the stable. Of course, you may well have to rely on a shed or even part of a room in the house. Nevertheless, with the tack room, the same stable rules apply. It must be dry and weatherproof and, if possible, kept reasonably warm. For, within this area, you will store the saddle, bridle, head-collar, rugs and quite an amount of your horse's food. For nuts, bran, oats, etc., galvanised dustbins serve best of all. The food you buy for your horse is going to be expensive. Paper and plastic sacks can and do fall over, wasting your money and making a mess, while the dustbin is a strong, stable article and, of course, prevents rats and mice attacking your foodstore. A saddle-horse or rack will be necessary to store your saddle tidily and hooks, or nails, on the wall for the bridle and head-collar are also essential. Do keep the tack room in a clean and well-ordered condition. Don't, just because you're tired, throw all that expensive gear on the floor. If you do, then in a short space of time you'll be paying a lot of money to replace it. In today's world, we all have to be conscious of security. And, even though the stable and tack room may be within sight of the house, they're not necessarily safe from thieves. Your horse and tack have probably cost a fair deal of money and it's very difficult to identify a saddle or bridle as belonging to you. Similarly, to prove that a stolen horse is yours can set quite a poser, although a relatively new system of freeze marking has offered a chance to prove ownership. The local riding school will almost certainly be able to tell you how and where this can be done. But to avoid these problems of theft, make sure that both stable and tack room are very firmly locked up when you're not around the place (and this may also well be a condition of your insurance policy).

This horse has been freeze marked with its own individual number to help the police locate it in the event of theft or straying.

Now whether you're short of space, money or perhaps both, it is nevertheless essential that you hold at least one week's adequate supply of bedding material, hay and hard food. Just remember what havoc an English winter can play with road conditions. Ice, snow and fog can make it virtually impossible for transport to move around for long periods of time and, while you're waiting to drive into the nearest town or, indeed, the nearest farm to collect your next supply, your horse could be going very hungry.

Have we convinced you that owning a horse is no bed of roses? It really is hard work, and it never lets up, but it's well worth the effort!

Horse clothing

What a lot of nonsense, you may imagine when you come to this section. And indeed, if the horse had been left in its natural state, the need for a wardrobe, for that indeed is what the horse now has to have, would be just that – a lot of nonsense. But over many centuries we have bred and adapted the horse to our needs and in doing so have removed quite a deal of the horse's own natural protection. In the case of the highly bred horse, the coat no longer grows as thick as it used to and therefore the horse becomes susceptible to chills and colds just as we humans do and the animal's need for protection and warmth is very similar to ours. But before we go on to explain those many items of clothing your horse will need, we have to allow the one exception: if the first horse or pony you buy has been used to spending his entire year out at grass, then he will be more than able to grow his coat according to the severity of weather he is experiencing. Of course, this rule only applies to the very hardy, and it is much more likely that the first horse you buy will be quite reasonably bred and therefore will not grow the amount of coat he will need when the winter weather starts.

The New Zealand rug

An absolute necessity for all horses that spend some of their time out to grass. Do buy the best you can possibly afford, for like your own mackintosh it protects you from the rain and it keeps you warm. Two basic types of this rug are available: the first has a sewn-on surcingle and two straps which attach from the inside of the rug across and between the hind legs to the opposite side and are secured by a metal ring just above the bottom corner of the rug. Make sure it fits securely and that there is no chance of it slipping when the horse is out in the field, even after he's had a good roll. Always take particular care when fastening the buckle and the straps. These are areas where the horse can chafe and become particularly uncomfortable. A close, secure fit is essential. Nothing must be able to get between

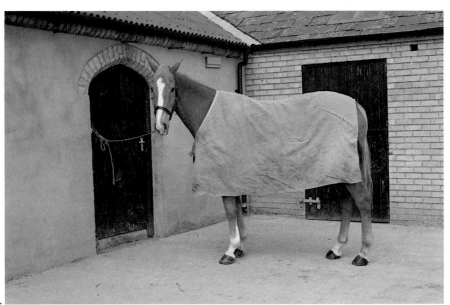

The New Zealand rug.

The jute rug.

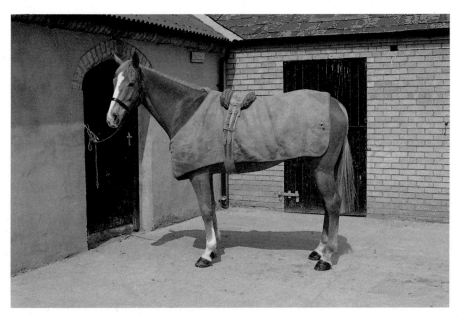

the rug and the horse's coat. Imagine just for a moment how uncomfortable it is when a stone gets into your shoe. Well it's the same with the horse; the same irritation, the same soreness is caused by something coming between the rug and the coat.

The second type of rug (shown in the picture) is the one we'd like to recommend. This has no roller at all, but relies on a good fit. It is actually cut and shaped to the body of the horse. It fits snugly around the neck and is much deeper than the previous type. This depth helps to keep the rug balanced and certainly gives extra warmth. The hind leg straps, instead of crossing over, loop around each other and return to the side they were attached to. This type of rug obviously has greater advantages over the previous one since there is no pressure on the horse's back from the roller. The horse is warmer and much more comfortable.

Keep your eyes on that rug. Yes, that's right – and we do mean it! For however well the rug is secured, it is at some point going to slip and without your *immediate* attention, at the best the horse is going to be very uncomfortable, at worst it is going to be frightened, and a frightened horse behaves stupidly and is often a danger to himself. We've emphasised the vital importance of the New Zealand rug when the horse lives out at grass, but it can also be used to good effect on a clipped and stabled animal. If the weather's a bit nippy, pop the rug on before turning the horse out in the field. It will keep him warm and reasonably clean.

The stable rug We are going to describe the variety of stable rugs that are available, but first of all, a spot of common sense. Imagine our normal winter weather with the paddock hock deep in mud; you've let your horse grow his full winter coat and you're bringing him in at night. Now there would be little point putting a rug over him when his coat was wet and muddy. Clearly he'd take more time to dry off and, when he had dried, the rug would sit very uncomfortably on the dried mud. And it is unlikely that he would need a rug if

The correct way to put on a blanket under a rug. This is a Polywarm rug held in place by a leather anti-cast roller. The leather-covered metal 'handle' on top of the roller prevents the horse from rolling right over on its back and thereby possibly getting stuck or 'cast' in its stable.

his coat has grown thick and you haven't groomed him too vigorously and removed the natural protective oils from his coat. A horse stabled by day and night, especially if he is clipped and well-groomed, will need a stable rug. The jute rug heads the list and is certainly the most popular. It is made of woven jute material and lined with a woollen blanket.

The rug is held in place with a jute or leather roller, the leather of course being far more expensive but, with good care and attention, will last much longer than the one made of jute. Do remember to keep your horse as comfortable as possible. Imagine how you'd feel with a leather strap around your back all day long. That's rather how the horse feels when a roller is fixed into place, so to help the horse and to ease the pressure of the roller, place a piece of thick sponge or folded blanket over the horse's back beneath the roller before you buckle it into position. It will certainly give the horse greater protection and greater comfort.

The Polywarm or Lavenham rug is also extremely popular for the simple reason that it is machine-washable. The rug is made of nylon quilted material with a cotton or nylon lining. They are light and very warm. The same sort of roller as used for the jute rug is used for the Polywarm or Lavenham, but some quilted rugs come with the roller attached or a roller in the same nylon material. These, from our experience, have proved unsatisfactory. Because of the nylon, the rug tends to slip and slide all over the place.

As the winter weather strikes colder, and particularly if your horse is clipped, he will certainly need some extra protection. He will feel the cold just as you do and without your help can do nothing about it. He will look very miserable and is likely to pick up the first available virus. A blanket under his stable rug will cheer him up immediately. Now these can vary from Whitney striped blankets, which look very attractive but are rather expensive, to an old blanket which has long outworn its use on your bed. The horse won't mind which one you use. The pictures show the right way to secure this extra blanket, the important object being to ensure that the blanket does not ruck up or slip and discomfort the animal.

Do remember when fixing the roller that its job is to hold the rug in place and not to squeeze the life out of the horse, and when fastening the rug at the front, allow enough room around the chest area for the horse to be able to lower his head without restriction. If the front fastening is too tight, the constant friction will rub the hair from his shoulders.

The day rug

The rugs we're going to mention now apply more to horses used in competition. There's no doubt that a day rug smartens up the horse and provides him with a good degree of warmth, as they are generally made of wool. But once again, use your common sense. If you're travelling your horse to and from shows in a horsebox, then you should use a day rug unless it is very hot. If your horse gets too hot, he'll fidget and this will make him become a restless traveller. He will also sweat up and will not arrive at the show looking very smart. If you do use a rug, make sure it is properly secured, for if it slips, the horse will panic and will remember this experience the next time you try to put him into his box. If your pocket can stand the strain, the horse travelling to the show can look exceedingly smart, since it's possible to match your day rug with rollers, tail guard, knee and hock boots.

The exercise rug

Called the paddock sheet in the racing world, this rug is made of wool and is worn under the saddle. Its function is to give warmth to a horse that's being ridden out. It is used especially on a clipped horse, when he is worked slowly, and not expected to sweat, and has a fillet string attached to it which runs under the tail to stop the rug from blowing or flapping about. It is cut straight down from the withers (with no front fastening) and loops around the girth.

The waterproof rug

Its name adequately explains it function. Used mainly for a horse waiting to appear in the show ring, it keeps the

A horse correctly dressed for travelling, with a smart woollen day rug, matching knee and hock boots, tail guard over a tail bandage and woollen leg bandages all round. Note the blue and white fillet string round the horse's quarters to prevent the back of the rug from blowing up. (Note also the correct way of holding the lead rope.)

The waterproof rug.

horse and tack dry but has the same problem experienced by humans wearing a raincoat – they can get rather hot and humid. It is made of rubberised or PVC material and can be put on when hacking to prevent the horse and the tack from getting wet, but remember they can cause the horse to sweat up.

The sweat rug

Naturally, a horse gets hot when he's been working hard and this is the time he is most likely to catch a chill. The sweat rug is designed to prevent that and to help the horse cool down without losing too much body heat. It is the most recognisable of all rugs, particularly for those who watch racing on the television. Our grooms have one ready to cover our horses' quarters as soon as we leave the show ring and, similarly, a stable lad at a racecourse will cover the horse's loins immediately it is in the unsaddling enclosure. A sweat rug looks rather like a large string vest, and it helps a hot horse to cool down properly as you walk him quietly around.

The sweat rug.

There is, however, one other application that we'd like to mention and would like you to make use of: perhaps you've been working your horse hard and he's come home hot and, providing it's not a *very* cold day, you might decide to give him a wash down. This you'll do with lukewarm water, paying particular attention to his face, ears, elbow and chest area, saddle patch and between his hind legs. Unless absolutely necessary, do not wash his loins. This is a particularly vulnerable area and the horse can catch a chill from a cold, wet loin area.

Having washed him down, cover him with a sweat rug and walk him around until he has started to dry. A horse that's been worked hard and then washed down will appreciate a bit of grass. Let him stop and eat as you walk around but generally keep him gently on the move.

The summer sheet

Another rug we recommend particularly for the horse's comfort is the summer sheet, a light cotton sheet in the usual rug shape with the normal front fastening. You can use it on cool summer days, on hot days to stop the coat standing up and when the horse is being particularly bothered by flies. No special roller is needed for this rug; use the normal stable roller.

If you can pick up an old summer sheet well past its best days, you can also use it as an under-rug. Put it beneath the blankets and stable rugs in the winter and you'll save on cleaning bills, because the sheet can be easily washed and dried, unlike the heavier rugs. It also adds that little bit of extra warmth, rather like wearing a vest in winter.

If your interest leads you towards the local show ring, then the summer sheet really comes into its own. On a hot and sunny day, throw a summer sheet over your horse to act as a sun shield. A hot horse standing around doing nothing soon becomes a bored horse, and that boredom may very well reflect on his performance when you eventually get him into the ring. So use your head and find some shade.

Bandages

Before we go through the business of bandages and boots, there is one thing we wish to emphasise: on no account tie the bandages too tightly. And how do you know if they're too tight? Very simple: when you take the bandage off, you will see lines scored around the coat of the horse. Tight bandages are bad for the horse's already rather poor circulation and are very uncomfortable. So, Rule Number 1: before you apply the bandage, use pieces of old blanket, special bandage pads or gamgee tissue to provide a comfortable buffer. Over these you can safely and firmly wrap the bandage. Stable bandages, essential protection for the travelling horse, are generally made of cotton or wool. Apply the bandage from just under the knee or hock down to the coronet, then secure the bandage with tapes, making a bow or knot on the outside of the horse's leg – never on the front or back of the leg where it might damage the tendons. Take particular care that the tapes are not pulled too tightly around the horse's leg, for apart from the obvious circulation problems tight tapes will cause, damage can be done to the tendons. To prevent these problems we're all in favour of what is a relatively recent development – bandages with velcro fastenings. We feel that bandages are preferable to boots for travelling, since boots, often simple pieces of foam-rubber or fleece-backed material with velcro fastenings, can more easily

The correct method of applying a stable bandage, with a firm, even pressure over the padding, taking it well over the fetlock joint and tying firmly but not too tightly on the outside of the leg. Add knee boots, if possible, for travelling, doing up the strap above the knee first and then the lower strap loosely so that the horse can still bend its knee.

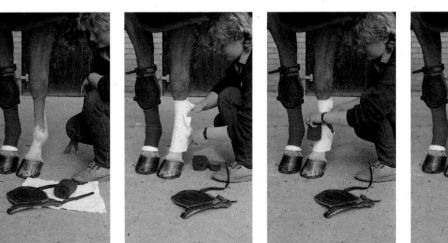

come undone. But if you can find some which fasten securely with straps, we would rather you used these until you were sure you could apply bandages correctly.

Obviously, bandages are used to give full protection to the travelling horse, but these bandages have a less obvious but nevertheless equally necessary use at home in the stable. After a physically hard day's work, you like to let your muscles relax in a warm bath. Now you can't run a bath for your horse, but by bandaging him up on a cold day after he's been working hard you can give him something of that sensation – immediate warmth and support just when he needs it. This of course only applies when the horse's legs have been clipped.

With a full winter coat he provides his own warmth. But it's not only after a hard day's work that he'll feel the cold. Like you, he'll be cold from just standing around. Again, if his legs have been clipped, buy a couple of pairs of large-sized leg warmers and slip them on to the horse's legs as he stands in his stable to provide him with extra warmth.

We don't feel that at this stage you should attempt to use exercise bandages. Your horse is unlikely to need them – the different types of boots we are going to describe are quite adequate for most purposes – and they can do more harm than good if they are put on incorrectly.

You should, however, know how to put on a tail bandage

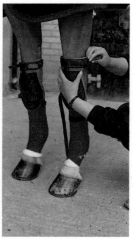

for travelling to protect the top of your horse's tail from
rubbing on the back of the horsebox. A tail in good
condition obviously helps the appearance of the horse, and
if he is constantly rubbing his tail hairs in every direction,
no amount of grooming will straighten them out again. The
best way to put on a tail bandage is to lift the tail, slide the
bandage right up under the dock and gradually bandage

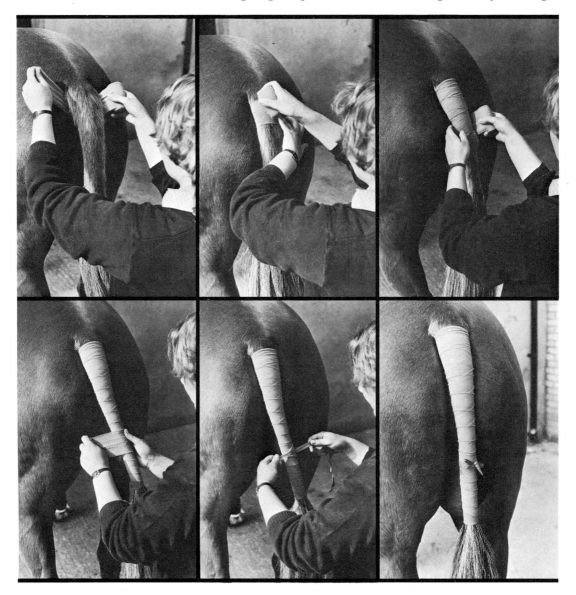

down to the end of the dock and up again, finally securing with tape. But remember, as with all bandages, don't tie it too tightly – and *never* leave a tail bandage on overnight, as this will certainly deaden the hairs of the tail and cause them eventually to fall out.

Since the horse will probably swish his tail around while travelling and cause the bandage to slip a bit, a tail guard over the top is useful. This generally fastens with three or four tapes or buckles around the dock and is secured with one long strap or tape to the roller holding the rug in place.

Boots

In the most simple language, some horses knock into themselves, and boots are used to prevent the obvious damage that this would cause. If your horse has this tendency, it will be known as a 'faulty action', but do make sure your horse really needs boots – don't clutter him up with unnecessary gear just because you think it looks smart.

Tendon Boots

These are worn on the front legs to support the tendons and protect the back of the front leg from blows by the hind leg. They can be made of leather – which is probably best – felt or a variety of artificial materials. Make sure, as with bandages, that you don't do the straps up too tight.

Overreach Boots

Tendon and overreach boots.

Generally made of rubber, they are sometimes known as bell boots, and are worn pulled over the hoof. These boots are particularly recommended for jumping, when the horse sometimes fails to pick up his front legs quickly enough to avoid overreaching or treading on the front heels from behind. The type with no fastenings can be hard to put on, and an old nylon stocking pulled over the horse's hoof first can help the boot to slide over more easily.

Knee Boots

The use of knee boots is a sensible precaution for a horse who is to be exercised on the road. It is very likely that the conditions will be slippery from time to time. It would be hoped that your horse never comes down on the road, but if he does, just imagine the amount of damage that he could do to his knees. A graze would be the least of his problems, though painful. A horse's bones are fragile and his knees particularly so. The use of knee boots is likely to prevent a major accident happening – so use them.

Bandaging and boots, as you will see, are from time to time very necessary, but we suggest that you spend time at your local stables talking to your riding master, watching how the bandages are applied and then, under expert supervision, do the job yourself. In this way, you'll gain confidence and, much more importantly, your horse won't be damaged. Many riding establishments run stable management lectures, and you would benefit greatly from attending these.

What you intend doing with your horse obviously dictates what you buy for him and with the rugs, the bandages, the boots, etc., time and experience will decide what you collect, but the items we're going to deal with next you will most certainly need.

The head-collar

Whether your horse lives in a stable or out at grass, or, indeed, a combination of both, the head-collar is vital. Without it he'll get nowhere and neither will you.

The picture on page 76 shows what it is and from that perhaps its use is obvious: the means to attach a lead rope enabling you to take the horse from point A to B and to tie him up. Once again, a variety of head-collars is available. The best and most expensive is made of leather, with the advantage that when cleaned and polished it looks very smart, and it will generally outlast all other varieties if properly cared for. Nevertheless, there is nothing wrong with the cheaper ones, these days generally made of nylon. Economy apart, they are quick to wash and dry and we're all using them. But whether your choice is leather or nylon, do take the head-collar off before turning the horse out into the paddock or field. The horse is an inquisitive creature and, in pushing his head into a forbidden area, the head-collar can easily get caught up. The nylon stitching would probably break, the leather would probably stretch and snap, but in any event the horse is going to panic, and that must at all times be avoided.

It's your job to make a good relationship with your horse, and if you need to turn him out with a head-collar on, as your only means of catching him up again, then we suggest that your relationship is not as good as it might be!

The lead rope Onto the head-collar you attach a lead rope. Once again, many varieties are available and you should buy what your pocket can afford, but they do take an enormous amount of wear. Horses chew them, they fray easily, so there's very little point in spending a lot of money on this particular item. We find that a plaited string lead rope is as good as any and if you can make one with a spare clip then that too will, in the long run, be good economy.

While we're on lead ropes, we want to hammer home something that has already been mentioned in the book but is all too often forgotten: DO NOT TIE YOUR HORSE UP BY HIS LEAD ROPE TO AN IMMOVABLE OBJECT. Always tie him up to something which will break, and the easiest way to achieve this is by tying a ring of single string to the post or whatever, and then attaching your lead rein to the string only. Now, if the horse is frightened, panics and pulls back, the string will snap, he'll be free and eventually caught up again. Just try to imagine the damage your horse might do himself if he couldn't get free. Worse still, in a way, is the horse tied up by his reins. We see this done all too often by young and old alike, and can only wonder what happened to their brains. Some horses do take fright easily, and if he's trapped with a leather bridle around his head and tied firmly by his reins to a post or rail, there's little he can do except pull and pull. Ultimately, the bridle may break, but before it does, imagine the harm that the horse will have done to his mouth.

Always stand on the left-hand side of your horse when you're leading him and *never* wrap the rope around your hand. If he should run off or bolt, what's going to happen to you? However, you can give yourself extra purchase on the rope by tying a knot at the bottom end, enabling your hand to slip through and have something firm to anchor on as a last resort. And how many times have we all seen an experienced rider trying to pull a reluctant horse along from the front? You'll never match his strength, so don't waste yours. Rather, stand at his shoulder and push him along, nudge him along, then with the end of your lead rope or a stick, just flick at his side with your left hand and encourage him forwards. Always think in terms of encouraging your horse in whatever you want him to do.

The bridle

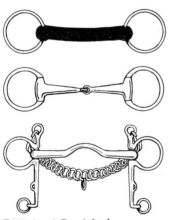

Bits: (top) Straight-bar rubber snaffle; (centre) Eggbut snaffle; (bottom) Pelham with curb chain.

We have already described the bridle in the 'Tack' section, but you will also need a bit. Once we start talking about the bit, we could take up a small book in itself. Which bit you ultimately use will be determined by a number of things: the character of the horse, possibly, the type of work you want him to do, whether his mouth is hard or soft, etc. – and you will get advice on the appropriate bit from your riding master. But we suggest that you keep your set simple, using a snaffle bit and therefore using a snaffle bridle, to which you might add a running martingale to offer a greater degree of control and discipline to the horse's head movements.

But if the horse you're thinking of buying looks like a walking tack shop when you first see him, there is a strong possibility that you might be looking at the wrong one for you.

The saddle

There is no doubt about the first rules in *this* case. The saddle *must* fit your horse, then it *must* fit you. This is one area where you can sensibly economise and go to the second-hand market. There is absolutely nothing wrong with a second-hand saddle just as long as it's in excellent repair. In fact, in this case, second-hand becomes a bonus, for if you buy a new saddle the leather is going to be stiff, as new leather always is, and you're going to spend a rather uncomfortable time working it into a comfortable condition. With a second-hand one, someone's done the job for you.

Now, although we heartily recommend a good quality second-hand saddle, we're not so keen on all those items that attach to the saddle coming from a second-hand source. Of course, the items we're talking about are the girth, which holds the saddle to the horse, the stirrup leathers and stirrup irons and the rubber treads. Now all these items of tack are vital to your safety and have got to be in excellent condition. Buy them new if you can, but if you can't, then keep your eyes very wide open for signs of wear and tear.

The numnah

This is a protective pad which goes onto the horse's back under the saddle. The market offers many varieties ranging from sheepskin to cotton. Later on, if you're going into competition, you can buy an expensive one, but for everyday riding, buy one which is easy to wash and dry, because the numnah will get dirty very quickly, since it's under the saddle that the horse sweats the most. Do wash the numnah very regularly – the horse's back will soon be made sore by a dirty and sweaty numnah. If your saddle is a tailor-made fit, then your numnah isn't absolutely necessary, but we think it offers a spot of comfort to the horse and a degree of warmth and we recommend them. Also it protects the underside of the saddle. We are quite happy to repeat that you like to be warm and comfortable – so remember – your horse likes to be warm and comfortable too.

Caring for your horse

You may be surprised to find out how much care a horse needs. He's a big, strong animal (you may say to yourself), and wild horses must be perfectly capable of looking after themselves without human beings dancing attendance on them day and night.

That's true, but think of the difference. Without a veterinary surgeon at hand, wild horses can sometimes lead painful lives and have early deaths. You'll want to do better than that for a horse that belongs to you.

Another thing about civilised life for a horse, as against life in the wild, is that there are many more hazards in civilisation against which you have to protect your horse. It's often in paddocks that picnickers leave jaggedly opened tins and pieces of broken bottle!

Finally, we expect a great deal of a trained horse. A wild horse can please himself, but your horse has to learn the part he must play in a very subtle and almost romantic relationship with his owner, you.

So take very seriously all the advice we give you. There really is a reason for everything. First, some general points . . .

In some ways, looking after a horse is like looking after a small child. Neither is equipped to explain to you in words that he has sustained a small injury or is beginning to feel unwell. The responsibility for vigilance is yours.

Horse and child both lack information about the dangers of their environment. Both will, through ignorance of the danger, cut themselves on broken glass.

Both will stray out of an unlatched gate and into a traffic-ridden road.

Neither can interrupt you in the middle of your favourite TV programme and say: 'I'm starving – isn't it supper-time yet?'

Both are easily frightened by things they don't understand (especially if sudden or unexpected), and easily confused by inconsistency in the way you treat them, or contradictions in the way you guide and instruct them.

Both rely on *you* to take the initiative in establishing and maintaining the relationship between you. Whether horse or child, you take notice of him . . . talk to him . . . show interest in him . . . touch him – patting and stroking the horse, and cuddling the child. Treat a horse like a bicycle, and it will respond as warmly as a bicycle.

General care We've already made clear the need for thorough grooming daily for the stable-kept horse, but there is more to it than just grooming. For example, you need to examine your horse first thing in the morning in case he has injured himself in any way during the night. If you turn your horse out to graze, which you should do daily if possible, you must check for any hazards – those we've already mentioned, like broken glass, and noxious plants and trees like hemlock, privet, yew, ground ivy, laurel, acorns, foxglove and ragwort, which should not be allowed to grow where your horse can reach them.

HEMLOCK

LAUREL   GROUND IVY   PRIVET

RAGWORT

FOXGLOVE

YEW

A grass-kept horse needs less grooming. In fact, when you don't ride him you need not groom him. As he lives largely in the open, he needs the natural grease and oils in his coat to protect him against the weather. In the very coldest weather, it is not wrong to allow him to stay plastered with mud (so long as the saddle area is clear), as this helps to keep him warm.

When you are picking out your horse's feet, which has to be done every day, you will also examine his shoes. Feet and their shoes are as important to a horse as they are to a ballerina; so you will check whether the shoes are so worn that they need replacing. Check if a shoe is loose, or even lost. Look also for 'risen clenches'.

The 'clench' is the end of the nail holding on the shoe, which projects from the wall of the hoof and is turned over to lie flush (carpenters clinch their nails – farriers clench them – it's the same thing). Sometimes the clenches rise and project, when they need immediate attention.

You will probably be surprised to find how often your horse needs the farrier, or blacksmith. It depends how much the horse does, and also what kind of work, but you can expect to give him a new set of shoes eight to ten times a year.

Shaping the hot shoe on the anvil so that it exactly fits the horse's foot;

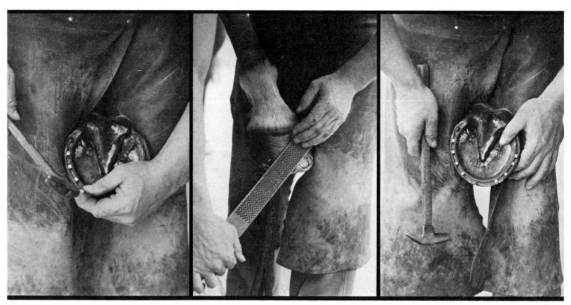

Banging in the nails;

Filing down the clenches, the ends of the nails protruding through the hoof, which have been turned over;

The new shoe in place. (The hole in the top left corner – the outside of the shoe – is for screwing in studs. You may eventually need to use these for jumping in certain ground conditions, but get advice on the correct type for your purpose first.)

Sometimes the farrier may be able to remove the shoes, trim the hooves, then refit the same shoes, which would be an economy. This really depends on how much road work has been done to wear the shoes down. If the horse is being rested, of course, he can go without shoes altogether. But the farrier will still be required to trim his feet from time to time to prevent splitting.

The farrier is not just the horse's shoemaker, he is the chiropodist as well. There's more to keeping feet in good condition than just putting shoes on. For example, the horn of the hoof grows continuously, just like your own toe-nails, and shoes prevent the natural wear hooves would get in the wild. So the farrier has to trim them periodically. Your horse could need a visit every four to six weeks.

Feeding your horse can clearly come under the heading of 'General Care', but we'll deal with this subject separately. As we've just been discussing the horse's physical well being, we'll now go on to consider the help you'll need from the veterinary surgeon.

The vet

This highly trained specialist is going to be the most important figure, apart from you, in your horse's life. With a bit of luck, he won't have to visit you too often, but when he does, it's going to be important.

So don't pick your vet out of the Yellow Pages. You might hit on one who's God's gift to goldfish with fungus but a dead loss when faced with an ailing horse. You need a specialist 'horse-doctor' and – as we keep on saying – there's nothing to beat personal *recommendation*. Your riding school or your horsey friends will tell you the names of vets they trust, and this gives you a first-class chance of getting the right vet first go.

Getting a good working relationship with your vet is important from several points of view. If your horse is sick or injured, it's no use just hoping that he'll get better of his own accord. On the other hand, you don't want to be calling the vet out every five minutes on false alarms or for small maladies you should be able to deal with yourself. You don't want to pay the vet for unnecessary calls, either!

To start with, put yourself in the vet's hands. He will probably say you can telephone him without hesitation whenever you are worried about the health of your horse. He will ask you to describe over the telephone the symptoms that are causing you anxiety, and then *he* will decide whether he ought to see the horse himself.

You will also want to consult him about first aid for your horse, and ask him to recommend a list of contents for the first aid box in your stable. Apart from the aspirin, antiseptic, sticking plaster and so on for your own use, he will probably agree that the basic essentials are:

Vet's telephone number
Sterilised crepe bandages
Roll of gamgee tissue
Penicillin wound powder
Antiseptic spray
Embrocation
Dettol
Pair of scissors
Cotton wool

Immediate first aid

Small cuts and scratches These occur all too frequently
and can be dealt with by you on the spot. But even so, a
horse with even the smallest cut or scratch that has not
been immunised against tetanus is in extreme danger. So
when you buy the horse, check whether or not it has had a
tetanus injection. Should the horse not have been
protected, then have the vet do the job as quickly as
possible. Deal with a small cut or scratch quickly too.
Wash the wound with warm, salty water (or you can use
Dettol water), then carefully pat the area dry. Dust the
wound with penicillin powder or use the antiseptic spray.
You'll obviously keep a careful eye on these small injuries
during the daily inspection, making sure the wound is
healing cleanly and repeat the operation until you're
satisfied the healing process is over.

A kick or blow The horse suffers the same kind of swelling
or bruising as humans. And the treatment is not that
different. Hose the bruised area frequently or, if on a leg,
apply a cold-water bandage or ice pack until the swelling
decreases and the soreness disappears. Soak a large piece
of gamgee tissue in cold water, then wring out the surplus
but still leave the tissue very wet. Bandage carefully but
firmly around the leg and when the bandage has dried up,
repeat the process until the horse recovers.

Colic The following symptoms will alert you to the
possibility of colic: the horse may seem restless, he might
be kicking or biting at his sides, he could be trying to get
down and will almost certainly be sweating up. Any of
these signs will tell you that *an immediate phone call to
the vet* is vitally important. While you are waiting for the
vet's arrival, keep the horse warm. Walk him gently
around the stableyard. On no account allow him to get
down and roll. Keep this up until the vet arrives and then
he'll take over.

A severe cut Such an injury is, of course, instantly
recognised by the amount of bleeding. It's likely that a vein

or artery has been damaged and the first thing you must do is endeavour to stop or at least check the bleeding. Bandage the wound with a clean pad of gamgee tissue. Tie the bandage as tight as you possibly can over the wound. Then, if possible, find the pressure point above the wound and bandage again there in exactly the way you would tourniquet a human wound. Phone the vet immediately and stress the urgency of the situation.

Feeding

Food is probably the most important single factor in the health and well-being of any living creature. We're still going to concentrate on the stable-kept horse but let's not forget for a moment the horse out at grass. In the summertime, when grass is good and plentiful, it's unlikely that he'll need very much extra food. However, during the winter months, he'll most certainly need hay morning and night. Give him as much hay as he can eat and also a supplementary feed, possibly nuts, during the day. These will keep him in good condition and help him to create his own warmth, vitally necessary to your horse during the winter. A hot meal at night would be extremely welcome to him. Also remember that if the weather is extremely wet – and it can go on, as we know, for days and days – bring the horse in to any form of shelter you have and dry him off as thoroughly as you can. It will allow him a little time to warm up and stop him getting too cold and miserable and losing condition. Horses can stand dry cold much better than wet.

Because grass is the horse's natural food, and hay is dried grass, the stable-kept horse's main item of diet is, not surprisingly, hay. His main feeds of the day will be given to him in a manger or bucket, but you will also feed hay – either in a hay net that you can hang on the wall of his box, on the floor or in a manger. A horse eats little and often, and he should be able to help himself to hay when he feels like it. A horse will get bored by himself, and a plentiful supply of hay will help him to pass the time with little snacks.

Hay on its own would be as monotonous a diet for horses

as potatoes on their own would be for humans; it would also be inadequate from a dietary point of view. So the hay must be supplemented by a number of other foods to give variety and to supply proteins, vitamins and other necessities. Remember to ask the horse's previous owner exactly what the horse was fed. Initially follow that and then consult your vet about your horse's diet, because the correct choice depends upon a variety of factors, such as the size of the horse and the work it has to do. Here we can only tell you in general what to expect when you go shopping for your horse's larder.

Some of the feeds you may get for your horse: (from left clockwise) hay, nuts, bran, barley, Equivite supplement, carrots, sugar beet.

You will probably give your horse some cereals, such as barley and maize; but be sparing with the oats. Oats are good food and the horses enjoy them, but they are great providers of energy and can make your horse inconveniently frisky. (The colloquial phrase, 'He's feeling his oats' reflects centuries of experience of oat-fed horses!)

There are other foods that the horse will find appetising. In rather smaller quantities they will add variety to his diet. These are apples, carrots (which must be sliced lengthways or fed whole – horses have been known to choke on a carrot chopped in rings), swedes, turnips, beetroot and other root crops, which must always be washed clean of mud.

Bran is another good food for a horse. Given as bran mash, it is also good for his bowels. If a horse is off-colour he may find his bran mash more appetising with some treacle or molasses in it.

Bran mash is simple to make. Put one scoop of bran into a bucket; add a good handful of oats or flaked maize; then, if you wish, a smaller handful of epsom salts. Onto this pour boiling water and mix until you have a crumbly consistency. Cover the top of the bucket with a doubled sack to seal it as much as possible and allow the mixture to steam in the bucket for 15-20 minutes. It will then be ready to feed to the horse. It's a particularly useful feed if the horse has been strenuously exercised, for instance out on a day's hunting. He finds it easy and light to digest and it has those necessary warming qualities. Also use this mash the night before the horse has a day off. It helps him to clear his system and protects him from the dangerous symptoms (of azoturia, or 'Monday morning sickness') of having too much energy-giving food in his system which he will not be utilising on his rest day.

Linseed mash or linseed jelly is good for the horse's health and helps to put a gloss on his coat. Sugar beet, which should be very well soaked for at least twelve hours before feeding, is a tasty and fattening addition.

Horse cubes are a manufactured product intended to bring a horse's diet up to a satisfactory nutritional level, and they contain protein, vitamins and minerals – rather like human diet supplements. But unlike the human diet supplements, cubes, or nuts as they are much more commonly known, are often fed entirely on their own as a kind of 'convenience food'. Or they can be used in addition to other foods.

The best nuts to feed alone are called 'complete nuts'. These have all the right ingredients mixed in them and are easy to feed to the horse. However, they do tend to be boring and it's as well to vary the diet as much as possible. The bag that holds the nuts will carry full directions on how to use them. Make sure these directions are followed.

It's as well to know what these basic foods do as well as what they're called. So the following lists some of the very basic foods and explains their function.

Bran

This is the outer coating of the wheat and is produced during the milling of flour. It's a laxative when used damp but becomes a binding agent when fed dry. Used as a mash, a sick or tired horse finds it very easy to digest. Like hay, bran must always have a sweet, fresh smell. As you would avoid musty smelling hay, similarly avoid musty smelling bran.

Barley

This cereal is very high in starch and therefore is used as a fattening food. Boil the grain whole until it bursts. Or, like oats, it may be fed rolled. Do not use too much of it in conjunction with nuts, since barley forms a prime constituent of all nuts and therefore the horse will have sufficient in his diet already.

Oats

These should be plump, clean and sweet smelling. Fed in moderation, they are likely to 'jazz up' horses, that's to say, make them very lively and larky. If this is not the effect required, then the oats can be boiled, which takes excess heating value out of them. Boiled oats can be fed to a sick horse as an appetizer. This cereal is fed in a bruised or cracked form only. *Don't feed whole oats to your horse.*

Flaked maize

This cereal is extremely high in starch. Half a pound a day will be plenty for a small horse. It functions well in adding flesh to the animal and helping to maintain good body heat, so it is a particularly useful winter feed.

All the above cereals are found in the compound mixture of nuts that we have described. So, therefore, do read instructions carefully and when using any of the nuts we recommend, don't overfeed with the cereals. But when working out your horse's diet, do remember he must have a variety of food and if you keep pumping him full of the same food day by day then your horse will become bored.

Golden rules of feeding

1 Feed your horse according to the work he has done and is going to do.
2 Always give him water before feeding.
3 Wait at least one hour before you ride your horse after feeding him.
4 Always feed good quality food.
5 Damp all feedstuffs down. (Hay may also be dampened for horses with a cough or wind problems.)
6 If you make his diet up of nuts alone, do make sure he has a very adequate water supply.
7 Always feed at regular times.
8 Feed little but often.
9 If the horse is hot and tired, do control his water intake. And feed him mash until he recovers.
10 This is simple hygiene but vitally important – wash the manger and feed buckets at least once a day.

As you become more experienced, your horse's diet will become a matter of common sense. For instance, if the horse is off work through sickness or just simply resting, then you wouldn't feed him the heating foods like oats. These will only excite him and make him impatient. Bran mash and plenty of hay is what he requires. Of course if the horse is sick, much like the human, something special goes down well. Prepare small, tasty feeds by adding sugar or molasses, carrots or anything that will tempt him to eat. If, when you're feeding your horse, you notice he's having difficulty chewing or the foods are spilling out of the sides of his mouth, he may have problems with his teeth. If a horse's teeth are too sharp, they tend to catch the sides of his mouth and this makes eating difficult for him. The vet should be asked to rasp his teeth at least once a year.

Also, do remember to buy food in quantities that you can use up within one month. There is little point laying in vast quantities even if you can afford to, for naturally, after a while, the food will tend to go off, become stale and musty. Always feed your horse food which is as fresh as possible.

What will your horse be like?

We've tried to make everything in this book useful to all readers in all circumstances. When we've mentioned 'your horse', we haven't really been thinking of any particular horse or any particular kind of reader. But now we want to turn your attention to a *very* particular horse – the first one that you are ever going to own.

It may be a long way off. You may have to ride a great many horses belonging to other people before you ever get one of your own. But you can start thinking about it *now*!

We have already said that you must buy a horse that fits you. In discussing the size of the horse, you will want to talk the language of the world of the horse – at present, the height of a horse is measured in 'hands' (though this will be replaced by metric measurements in the fairly near future).

A hand is four inches, or a fraction more than ten centimetres. When a pony is described as '11.2 hands', it does not mean (as you would expect) '11 hands and one fifth of a hand'; that dot is not a decimal point, but simply separates complete hands from the odd inches. That is to say, 11 hands means 44 inches measured at the highest point of the withers. So 11.1 hands means 45 inches; 11.2 hands, 46 inches; 11.3 hands, 47 inches.

There aren't any 11.4 hands because that would be 48 inches (and that, of course, is 12 hands). These five measurements, from 11 hands to 12 hands, convert to the metric 111cm, 114cm, 117cm, 119cm and 122cm to the nearest whole centimetre. This, by the way, would be the height of a rather small pony – only four feet tall.

We hope that, at some point, you will be wanting to show or jump your horse or pony in the show ring, and it's at that point that the height of the horse becomes vitally important because all classes into which you may enter your horse will be governed by the height of the animal. So, if you're thinking in terms of the local show, be conscious that the horse you are buying (a) can do the job properly but (b) is of the right height and size for you.

We would like to stress again here the importance of the

Both these animals are suitable types and sizes for their novice riders. They are well-mannered, going forward freely and calmly, and are unlikely to get upset if the rider makes a mistake occasionally.

age of the horse and the sensible principle that the less experienced the owner is, the more experienced the horse should be!

There would not be much sense in our advising you to aim for a particular type or breed of horse. Your very first purchase will have to be made from a short-list of horses that are available to you at the time – through personal knowledge, through recommendation, or through advertising in the specialist periodicals. However, you're going to be talking to knowledgeable people, and you do want to know something of what you are talking about, so you ought to be acquainted with the language in use. You should therefore have a working knowledge of points of the horse, colours, markings and breeds.

The points of the horse

You need to study the picture here. Some of the information will be completely obvious – as technical terms, 'eye' and 'ear', for example, will give you no trouble. But someone selling you a horse might refer to his 'coronet', and you might (not unreasonably) start inspecting the top of his head. If you look at the picture you will see why this could lead to a certain amount of embarrassment. It's worth doing a bit of homework with the help of the picture; it really won't take long to be completely certain of the difference between a fetlock and a pastern, and to refer to croup or gaskin as naturally as you already talk about mane or tail.

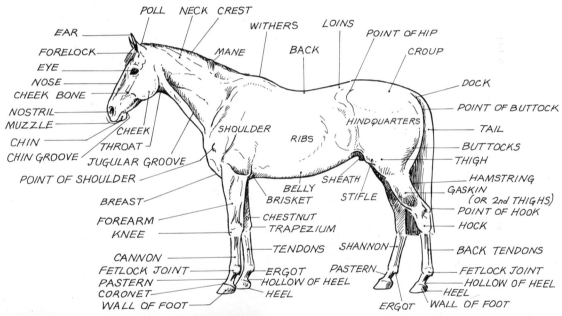

Markings

A horse's 'markings' are clearly identifiable patches of white which play an important part in linking a horse with his proper name and record.

Some of these markings are found on the legs: a white marking from hoof to knee or hock is known as a 'white stocking'. If the marking stops before it reaches the hock, it is then known (reasonably enough) as a 'white sock'. You will immediately recognise a 'white pastern', a 'white fetlock' and a 'white heel' – provided you've done your homework on the 'Points of the horse' picture.

A white stocking.

A white sock.

A white pastern.

A white heel.

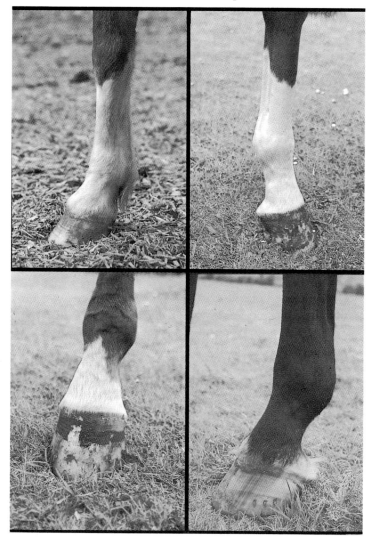

Markings on the head – and remember that they're always white – are as follows:

Star. Any definite mark on the forehead counts, even though the shape and size may vary. A few white hairs in that region of the head do not qualify.

Stripe. A narrow marking running down the face no wider than the surface of the nose bone. Therefore, you can talk in terms of a broad or narrow stripe and refine the description further by stating whether it inclines to the left or right.

Blaze. A broad marking covering all the forehead between the eyes and extending down the face beyond the nose bone to the muzzle.

White face. Very much what the name says. The mark covers the entire face and extends round to the mouth.

Snip. A small mark not connected with any of the others named. It's found between or in the region of the nostrils.

White muzzle. Here the mark covers both lips and moves up to the region of the nostrils.

A star.

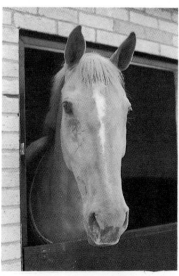

Sunorra has a white stripe.

Colour

It may seem strange to give special attention to the question of colour, but there are two good reasons for this. First, the terms used are not always what you'd expect. For example, white horses don't exist (except in the whisky advertisements) – a horse that looks white is always called a 'grey'.

On any level, horses aren't cheap but at top level they are incredibly expensive. They are bought and sold, move from country to country and the only identity card they have is the colour and markings they were born with. That's why the authorities are now looking for a uniformly higher standard of identification and why we have paid particular attention to colours and markings.

Black. Black hair throughout the coat allows no pattern other than white markings. The mane, tail and limbs are also all black.

Brown. The coat is a mixture of black and brown hair. The limbs are black, as are the mane and tail.

Bay-brown. The main colour on this one is brown. The difference being that he has a bay muzzle but the same black limbs, mane and tail as the brown.

Bay. The bay offers a great variety of brown shades from a dull, reddish colour to a yellowish colour nearing the chestnut. Black mane, tail, limbs as the bay/brown and brown, but here the ears are tipped with black.

Chestnut. The colour here is a mixture of gold hair and, depending on the intensity of the mixture, the horse is either a light or dark chestnut. What's known as the 'true chestnut' has a mane and tail the same basic colour as the coat but of a darker intensity. But horses with flaxen manes and tails still count as chestnuts.

Grey. The coat is a mixture of white and black hair on a black skin. The mixture present will determine whether you have a light or dark grey. As the horse ages, the coat becomes lighter in colour. Within the grey range there is a

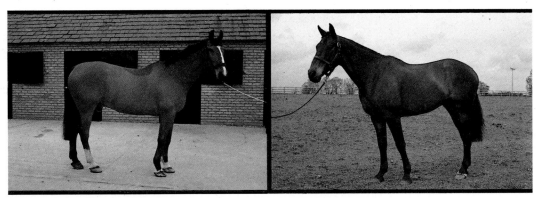

Corunna Bay, one of the famous
horses which Steve rode, was a bay
with a white blaze.

A bay-brown.

One of the many varieties of grey,
this horse is a dappled grey.

A strawberry roan.

A palomino. Once his summer coat
is completely through, his whole
body will be the colour of the hair
on his shoulder in this picture.

term, 'flea bitten', which generally means there's a third colour present.

Roans. Quite a few of these. The difference is determined by the basic permanent body colour.

Blue roan. Body colour here is black or brown/black with a mixture of white hair which gives a blue tinge to the coat. On the legs, from the knees down, black hair predominates.

Bay or red roan. Body colour here is bay or bay-brown with a mixture of white hairs which give the coat a reddish tinge. Lower legs as with the blue roan.

Strawberry or chestnut roan. The body colour here is chestnut with the white hairs present.

Blue dun. The skin colour is black, the hair colour pale black evenly carried across the body. The mane and tail are black and a black band running along the spine may be present.

Yellow dun. The skin colour is again black with this time a pale yellow hair evenly distributed across the body. Again it's possible to find the black spinal band present.

Cream. The body coat is an all-over cream colour. The eyes often have a pinkish or blueish appearance due to deficient pigmentation in the iris.

Piebald. The coat consists of large, irregular patches of black and white. The contrast between the two colours is generally very sharp.

Skewbald. Exactly the same as the piebald with any choice of colour making up the patches except black.

Palomino. A golden colour, nicely described to us once as the colour of a new penny. Lighter or darker shades are permitted. The tail and mane must be white.

Appaloosian. The body colour is grey covered with a mosaic of black or brown spots.

Riding horse breeds and types

The thoroughbred

Acknowledged to be one of the most elegant and beautiful horses in the world, the thoroughbred has a fine head set on an elegant neck with good, sloping shoulders, a deep girth, powerful quarters and strong legs. The breed was evolved in England by crossing Eastern stallions with native mares. In the seventeenth and eighteenth centuries, the racehorse enthusiasts of England soon produced the fastest horse in the world. Three famous stallions are accepted as being the founding fathers of the breed. They are the Byerley Turk, imported in 1689, the Darley Arabian, imported in 1705, and the Godolphin Arabian, imported in 1728. The English thoroughbred is exported all over the world. Wherever racing is popular, the English thoroughbred is established. It is also used to improve other breeds. Their quality and presence is at a premium. The horse generally stands 16 hands or thereabouts but, of course, height can vary a great deal. It is successful at all sorts of equestrian events where courage and stamina are required, but it must be stated that the thoroughbred would not be a sensible first horse for an inexperienced rider. The usual colours are bay, brown and chestnut, although they may also be grey or black.

A Thoroughbred stallion.

127

The hunter

This is not an exact breed, but an English hunter is generally, and perhaps at best, a cross between the thoroughbred and the Irish Draught. It is a horse of generally good conformation, well capable of carrying a rider for several hours over a variety of countryside and any obstacles which may present themselves. In show classes, the horses are judged according to the best weight they are suited to carry (i.e. lightweight up to $13\frac{1}{2}$ stone, middleweight up to $14\frac{1}{2}$ stone and heavyweight over $14\frac{1}{2}$ stone) and great importance is placed on the horse's conformation. The hunting season extends through the late autumn and winter months, so the better the conformation of the horse, the more likely he will be to see the season through in a sound condition. Again, not a horse we would recommend for a beginner because of the high proportion of thoroughbred blood.

A good sort of working hunter.

The Irish Draught

As the name clearly suggests, this horse originated in Ireland. It is a horse whose chief value is in producing good competition horses, particularly when the mare is put to a thoroughbred stallion. The best examples of this breed have good, sloping shoulders and strong, sound legs. The action is particularly pleasing, being free and straight. Also the breed normally possesses a bold, natural jump. Sadly, during the First World War the breed suffered serious losses as the best mares were requisitioned for use by the army. The usual colours are grey, bay, brown and chestnut. It's a breed we would particularly recommend for the novice rider.

A good example of an Irish Draught mare.

Mulgrave Supreme, a Cleveland Bay stallion owned by Her Majesty The Queen.

The Cleveland Bay

This breed originated, as again the name suggests, in Cleveland, Yorkshire. It's an extremely handsome horse with a large, convex head set on a longish neck with good shoulders, deep girth and a strong, fairly long back. The legs are short, with plenty of bone and good, strong feet. The coat is always of a bay colour and the horse stands around 16 hands. It's an ideal riding horse but can also double up as a carriage or driving horse. It possesses an intelligent, sensible temperament matched with strength and stamina. The breed benefits by being crossed with a thoroughbred to produce an all-purpose animal.

129

A fine example of a cob.

The cob

This type is identified by a short-legged, stocky body. It's not a tall horse, standing around 15 hands. It has a small, neat head and thick, arched neck with a short, deep body and ample hind-quarters. A good cob provides a comfortable ride and is blessed with a placid, obedient temperament. For an elderly or nervous rider, a cob makes an ideal companion and is also suitable for all the family, for what he lacks in speed, he will make up for in handiness and manners.

A top quality Hanoverian mare, Wadacre Trudi, at 3 years old. Her strong, correct limbs and very strong back (indicated by the well-carried tail) are characteristic of a good Warm-Blood horse and the powerful hocks are particularly important in producing the active, athletic performance for which her breed is noted. (*Photo: R. McEwen*)

The Hanoverian

This is a German breed of well-made, big, strong, upstanding horses of good conformation. By some they are thought to be a little plain but they have a great amount of courage and are generally active and bold. Therefore, it's not a horse that we can recommend for the inexperienced rider. They require a lot of work and have a strong will and temperament, which finds its home most happily in the show-jumping ring.

The leopard-spotted Appaloosa stallion, Klaus, National Champion since 1977.

The Appaloosian

A breed of saddle horse which originated in North America. It was initially bred by the Red Indians who inhabited the Paloux Valley until 1877. The breed descended from horses brought up from South America by the Spanish Conquistadors during the sixteenth century. It's an extremely popular horse in America and is becoming increasingly so in England. As an all-round saddle horse, it's noted for its agility and good disposition. It possesses speed, stamina and can jump well. But again, perhaps not the first horse for the novice to buy.

The Arab

Again, the name suggests the origins of this breed, which is one of the oldest and purest in breeding records. The horse possesses extreme beauty and refinement and is easily

131

distinguished by dished nose, broad forehead, large eyes and small muzzle. The head is carried high on a compact, muscular body. The legs are slender but extremely strong. The mane, tail and coat are of a silky texture. The tail is also carried high and the horse, when moving freely, displays its tail in a fan-like fashion. The breed is known for its power of endurance and ability to carry weight despite its small size. It rarely stands more than 15 hands high. It's becoming well-liked as a long-distance riding horse but bear in mind its breed in terms of a very high spirit. We do not recommend it to the inexperienced rider.

The Arab stallion Sky Crusader, British National Champion and sire of champions at home and abroad, has been raced, hunted and shown under saddle as well as in hand. (*Photo: Ross Laney*)

Riding pony breeds

The Connemara

This was a native of Ireland although it's now bred extensively in England. The breed has had, over the centuries, various strains of thoroughbred, Arab and Clydesdale blood added to it. This has improved and refined the breed to the point where it has now developed into a largish, good, all-round riding pony which suits most purposes. It stands between 13 and 14.2 hands, and is a sturdy animal with a good free action. It possesses a quality head on a good length of neck and has a deep girth with good, sloping shoulders. A straight back, well-developed quarters, good legs with plenty of bone and extremely good feet are among its many attributes. The breed is sure-footed and agile. This, matched with a kind nature, makes it the finest type of first pony for an inexperienced young rider. There's a large variation of colour, moving from grey, bay, black to dun or brown.

A Connemara pony.

133

The Dartmoor

This pony comes from the famous moor in the West of England where the breed has lived and flourished for thousands of years. In its domesticated state, it has developed into an ideal young child's first pony. It is small and narrow and carries its head quite high, is sensible, sure-footed and is possessed of a very kind nature. It also has a natural jump. The pretty head is dominated by a large eye and sharply pricked ears. It has a good front and sloping shoulders set on a short, compact body with good legs and feet. The usual colours are black, bay and brown with white markings. The height is never more than 12.2 hands and, as we said, a pony we recommend for the very young beginner.

A typical Dartmoor, one of the breed's top stallions. (*Photo: Carol Gilson*)

A typical Exmoor mare from the Anchor Herd. (*Photo: John Keene*)

The Exmoor

Another old West Country breed, this one going into the records of Doomsday Book in 1085. Of course, the breed is much older, as fossilized remains tend to prove. A fossilized jaw bone of exactly the same shape as that of the Exmoor pony has been found with the beginnings of a seventh molar. This is found in no other horse or pony, suggesting that the Exmoor breed could be one of the very first. It's a tough, strong, hardy little chap. It has great endurance, intelligence and independence. These aspects of its character require extremely correct handling or the animal becomes wilful. The height reaches no more than 12.2 hands and the colours are generally bay, brown or dun but with no light markings. Distinguishing features include a mealy muzzle and similar coloured markings around the eyes, underbelly and thighs. The pony has a short, thick head set on a similar neck, a short back, powerful quarters, short legs with plenty of bone and good, hard feet. It also has a unique feature which is called the toad eye. The eyes, in fact, have top lids which give them a hooded look. The ears are short and thick, the coat is by nature extremely close and short and if left unclipped seems to be virtually waterproof. It can make a good child's pony if properly trained but since it's extremely strong and can easily bear the weight of a full-grown man, it's perhaps best left alone as a first pony.

A good example of a New
Forest pony, Mudeford
Robin.

The New Forest

There's perhaps more of a mix in this breed than most
others. Certainly Welsh mares have been introduced into
this forest breed as well as several others. It's also well-
known that thoroughbred stallions have helped to improve
the breed, so it's rather difficult to define it in terms of
specific height, since it can range from 12.2 hands to 14.2
hands and can be of any colour with the exception of
skewbald or piebald. One of the most popular ponies, they
are sure-footed, have a good action which comes from good
sloping shoulders, and straight movement. They possess
plenty of bone, a short back, strong quarters and good feet.
They often have a large head set on rather a short neck.
They are excellent family ponies and most suitable for
riding or driving, since they have a generous, docile
temperament and are easily handled by children.
Thoroughly recommended for the beginner.

The Shetland

Once again, the name of the breed tells us where it came from. Now, of course, the Shetland pony is bred extensively all over Great Britain and in many other countries in the world. But, when it was first domesticated on the Shetland Isles, it was used primarily by the crofters. It carried peat, was used as transport, either being ridden or pulling carts. And in the middle of the nineteenth century, it was also used as a pit pony, as, being so short, yet strong, it made an ideal companion for the miner below ground. The height varies from 38 to 42 inches, and the animal is extremely well built, strong and hardy. The most prevalent colour is black, though any colour can occur. These handsome little characters are also noted for an abundance of mane and tail hair. They provide an ideal first pony for the very young child (and can be seen between the shafts of a scurry demonstrating their strength, speed and manoevrability – always great fun at the shows and we enjoy watching them).

The Shetland.

The Welsh Mountain

A beautiful and extremely popular native breed. They've inhabited the mountains and moorlands of Wales since pre-history times. The Romans certainly took note of them and used them. The breed is intelligent, courageous, kind and gentle and, like the Shetland, provides a fine first pony for a young child. It too is suited to harness work. It possesses a fine, slightly dished head, large, wide-spaced eyes and small, pricked ears. It has an alert outlook, is sound, tough and hardy. It has an intelligent head and a good, sloping shoulder with compact body and short, strong legs with good feet. It is often grey but can be any colour with the exception of piebald and skewbald, and in height it can go up to 12.2 hands.

A Welsh Mountain mare.

The Welsh pony

This breed comes from crossing the Welsh Mountain pony and the Welsh Cob, with just a touch of thoroughbred blood for good measure. It is used for shepherding in the

Welsh hills and its characteristics are much the same as the Welsh Mountain pony. There is not so much knee action, they are courageous, intelligent, and height is limited at 13.2 hands. Colours exactly the same as the Welsh Mountain pony.

A most attractive example of the Welsh Section C pony of cob type, Synod Roger.

The palomino

This is a colour type and *not a breed,* but we have included it here because it is now recognised as a colour by the British Horse Society and there are official classes for palominos at many shows. The colouring can occur in a number of different breeds and, at its finest, the coat should look like a newly minted gold coin. But it still holds the palomino name with a coat either three shades lighter or three shades darker. We emphasise that the mane and tail must be white, and any variation disqualifies the pony as a palomino. The palomino foal may be born pale but then darkens with age. The final colour does not 'set' until the horse is approximately six years of age. There is no failsafe breeding method of producing the palomino colour. At best it is rather hit and miss, but just for interest here are crosses likely to produce the required colour: two palominos crossed; a chestnut crossed with a palomino; a chestnut with an albino; and a palomino crossed with an albino. This colour pony has become increasingly popular over the years.

139

Now, is there anything else we have to tell you?

The only possible answer is: 'Yes and No.' Yes – we could fill twenty books the size of this one with all the information we've collected in two lifetimes with horses. As it is, we suggest you look at the book list we've compiled for you, and consult the wisdom of other authors. Or perhaps a better way of spending your time is to go and learn *with* the horses, rather than sit and read *about* horses.

Our purpose has been to infect you with our own enthusiasms . . . to give you an understanding of all that lies ahead of you . . . and, perhaps, to help you replace the diffidence of the uninformed novice with the self-confidence of a natural resident in the great world of the horse!

Good luck!

Book List

The Encyclopedia of the Horse (Octopus)
R.L.V. ffrench Blake, *Elementary Dressage* (Warne)
Captain M.H. Hayes FRCVS, *Veterinary Notes for Horse Owners* (Stanley Paul)
Janet W. Macdonald, *The Right Horse: An Owners' and Buyers' Guide* (Methuen)
W. Müseler, *Riding Logic* (Methuen)
Peter D. Rossdale FRCVS, *The Horse from Conception to Maturity* (J.A. Allen)
Peter D. Rossdale and Susan M. Wreford, *The Horse's Health from A to Z* (David & Charles)
Peter C. Smith, *The Design and Construction of Stables* (J.A. Allen)
Diana R. Tuke, *Feeding Your Horse* (J.A. Allen)

Index

Numbers in italics refer to illustrations.